Cambridge Elements

Elements in Contemporary Performance Texts
edited by
Fintan Walsh
Birkbeck, University of London
Duška Radosavljević
Royal Central School of Speech and Drama, University of London
Caridad Svich
Rutgers University

MOVEMENT, TEXT, PERFORMANCE

Paul Allain
University of Kent

Shaftesbury Road, Cambridge CB2 8EA, United Kingdom

One Liberty Plaza, 20th Floor, New York, NY 10006, USA

477 Williamstown Road, Port Melbourne, VIC 3207, Australia

314–321, 3rd Floor, Plot 3, Splendor Forum, Jasola District Centre,
New Delhi – 110025, India

Cambridge University Press is part of Cambridge University Press & Assessment,
a department of the University of Cambridge.

We share the University's mission to contribute to society through the pursuit of
education, learning and research at the highest international levels of excellence.

www.cambridge.org
Information on this title: www.cambridge.org/9781009684286

DOI: 10.1017/9781009684279

© Paul Allain 2026

This publication is in copyright. Subject to statutory exception and to the provisions
of relevant collective licensing agreements, no reproduction of any part may take
place without the written permission of Cambridge University Press & Assessment.

When citing this work, please include a reference to the DOI 10.1017/9781009684279

First published 2026

A catalogue record for this publication is available from the British Library

A Cataloging-in-Publication data record for this Element is available from the Library of
Congress

ISBN 978-1-009-68428-6 Hardback
ISBN 978-1-009-68425-5 Paperback
ISSN 2753-2798 (online)
ISSN 2753-278X (print)

Cambridge University Press & Assessment has no responsibility for the persistence
or accuracy of URLs for external or third-party internet websites referred to in this
publication and does not guarantee that any content on such websites is, or will remain,
accurate or appropriate.

For EU product safety concerns, contact us at Calle de José Abascal, 56, 1°, 28003
Madrid, Spain, or email eugpsr@cambridge.org

Movement, Text, Performance

Elements in Contemporary Performance Texts

DOI: 10.1017/9781009684279
First published online: March 2026

Paul Allain
University of Kent
Author for correspondence: Paul Allain, paa@kent.ac.uk

Abstract: This Element argues that movement, overseen by a movement director, is vital for theatre-making. It can support actors with characterisation and playing others responsibly and ethically, for scripted and non-scripted tasks: from dances to fights, from parades to murders, or other human behaviour. Movement directing is an increasingly common role as it helps forge an ensemble and build 'worlds' on stage, and plays a crucial part in shaping how actors work with and in space. The Element's autoethnographic approach draws on the author's movement direction for ten productions in the UK, most with director Katie Mitchell, based on his research into and experience with Gardzienice Theatre Association, Poland, from 1989. The Element offers a perspective that is missing in accounts of Mitchell's oeuvre and much British movement scholarship by examining the influence of the Grotowskian lineage on British theatre and by discussing voice work and text delivery, something often overlooked.

This Element also has a video abstract:
www.cambridge.org/ECTX_Allain_abstract

Keywords: movement, text, performance, acting, directing

© Paul Allain 2026

ISBNs: 9781009684286 (HB), 9781009684255 (PB), 9781009684279 (OC)
ISSNs: 2753-2798 (online), 2753-278X (print)

Contents

Introduction: Movement, Text, and the Polish Tradition   1

1 Enacting Cultural Difference   11

2 Making Worlds on Stage   30

3 Moving as a Creative Tool: Text, Voice, Music, and Death   43

Conclusion: Lessons from Polish Practice   58

References   62

Introduction: Movement, Text, and the Polish Tradition

This Element has arisen from my research into Polish theatre, movement, and actor training, which began in autumn 1989 when I started my PhD at Goldsmiths College, University of London. My doctorate was about the Polish theatre company Gardzienice Theatre Association, which I first saw in 1988, performing in the medieval hall at Dartington College, Devon, UK. I subsequently took a short workshop with them on the South Wales coast in April 1989, both activities organised by the Centre for Performance Research. At that time, almost nothing was written in English about their work. Their visit to the UK caused a stir and initiated further interactions, including my PhD. I visited Gardzienice village briefly in the summer of 1989 and then stayed for a longer period that autumn for doctoral fieldwork. In November, the Berlin Wall fell, and everything changed.

My research methods quickly evolved from outsider observation to include what is now commonly referred to as participant observation using practice research, as I trained and rehearsed with the company regularly. I donned a large monk's habit and hobnail boots and sang in the choir that was an integral part of *Avvakum* (originally 1983 but still in repertoire), which we presented in December in the converted former Arian chapel in Gardzienice. I later became even more immersed, in projects in Italy, Poland, Ukraine, the UK, and Japan, singing in the chorus of another performance, *Carmina Burana* (1990). I conducted Reconnaissances and Expeditions. This activity is documented and analysed in the book based on my PhD (Allain, 1997).

Other British practitioners also found their way to this tiny village in Southeast Poland, including director Katie Mitchell, to whom I had introduced the company. We had met through a mutual friend from the University of Oxford, as I recount in 'Stumbling around Polish Theatre with Katie Mitchell: a Personal Reflection' (*Contemporary Theatre Review*, 2020: 260–264). So began a collaboration that this Element will examine.

My focus is on how movement relates to text and performance, referencing my work as a movement director on ten productions, including eight with Mitchell. These professional engagements happened alongside and then continued after my PhD. In chronological order, the Mitchell productions that I analyse, some quite briefly, are: anon, *Arden of Faversham*, Classics on a Shoestring, Old Red Lion Theatre, London, 1990; Maxim Gorky, *Vassa Zheleznova*, Classics on a Shoestring, Gate Theatre, London, 1990; Sh. An-sky, *The Dybbuk*, Royal Shakespeare Company (RSC), The Pit, Barbican, London, 1992; John Arden, *Live Like Pigs*, Classics on a Shoestring, Royal Court Upstairs, London, 1993; Henrik Ibsen, *Ghosts*, RSC, The Other Place,

Stratford-upon-Avon, 1993; William Shakespeare, *Henry VI: The Battle for the Throne*, RSC, The Other Place, Stratford-upon-Avon, 1994; Githa Sowerby, *Rutherford and Son*, Royal National Theatre (RNT), The Cottesloe, 1994; and Ernst Toller, *The Machine Wreckers*, RNT, The Cottesloe, 1995. I worked on all these as a movement director. I will also examine two other productions where I led movement work: Mikhail Bulgakov's *Heart of a Dog* (Major Road Theatre Company, Bradford, and UK national tour, 1991) and the much later amateur production of Christopher Marlowe's *Massacre at Paris* (Fourth Monkey/The Marlowe Theatre, Canterbury Cathedral Crypt, Canterbury, 2014).

Influences

Mitchell and my collaboration arose from a shared interest in how to integrate into British practice techniques and rehearsal and training processes from Russia and Eastern Europe, and Gardzienice in particular. Gardzienice's approach, described in my 1997 book, includes the key concepts of 'mutuality' and 'musicality' in an intensely physical and vocal training. This interest was explained during an RNT Platform discussion between Mitchell and Genista McIntosh after the first night of *Rutherford and Son* (Platform, 1994). McIntosh was participating in her capacity as Executive Director of the RNT, a position she held from 1990 to 1996. She also knew Mitchell from her previous connection to the RSC, most notably when Associate Producer in 1990.

Almost half of the 45-minute Platform focused on influences from Eastern Europe and Russia on Mitchell's practice. This was returned to in the Question-and-Answer section, where attendees asked about our production of *The Dybbuk* from two years before. Benjamin Fowler, author of a book on Mitchell's directing (*Katie Mitchell: Beautiful Illogical Acts*, 2021), does not refer to the Platform there, but he examines this influence and its origins in detail. He mentions Mitchell's Winston Churchill Memorial Trust Award that enabled her to travel to Tbilisi, Moscow, and then Poland, starting in 1989. In the Platform, Mitchell describes how she 'discovered [...] an extraordinary Grotowski-style theatre company [...] inspiring a lot of the work I have done'. This 'eventually led to the RSC agreeing for this wacky avant-garde physical company to come and work with their actors twice' in 1991 and 1992: 'Grotowski meets talking heads' (Platform, 1994). This 'Grotowski-style company' was Gardzienice.

The conversation touches on questions at the heart of this Element. McIntosh presses Mitchell about this influence, noting how 'visible' it was in the early work, which had a 'very distinctive character'. Mitchell responds jokingly by summarising this as 'a lot of Bulgarian wailing', but then replies more seriously, with specific reference to *Arden of Faversham*. *Arden*, as we called it, was our first collaboration, for which I was responsible for 'movement and physical training'. This was under the auspices of Classics on a Shoestring, a company Mitchell and I had set up:

> we decided that we wanted to see where the meeting ground was between this extraordinary physical training that we had been through and the text-based work of the British acting school – and of course there wasn't a meeting ground and it took us at least 4 weeks to find out [...] There came a point when it became clear that the marriage between those two traditions – there wasn't going to be one, and really we would be better to do something different. (Platform, 1994)

Directly addressing me in the audience during the event to ask whether I agreed with her, Mitchell goes on to say that 'We resolved it and did something different that was ok' (Platform, 1994). I commented but did not answer directly.

It seems obvious now that no binding 'marriage' was ever going to happen in our first production, though some critics admired our bravery and others described it in the highest terms. In *Time Out*, Nicola Robertson wrote that it was 'a fascinating and successful experiment which blends the techniques of Polish theatre practice with a classic English dramatic text [...] Highly recommended'. Katherine Wearing in *City Limits* believed it 'works like a dream' (both 1990). Others were critical or mocking even. Desmond Christy in the *Guardian* showed his ambivalence, stating that 'Katie Mitchell and Paul Allain have directed their actors to roll in the soil when appropriate. Mitchell and Allain have been visiting Eastern Europe, and presumably, that is where they developed notions that theatre should make use of all of the senses' (1990). Quentin Letts suggested that 'East European theatrical theories are usually best confined to the coffee bars of redbrick universities' (*Daily Telegraph*, 1990). Perhaps these reviews say more about the relative conservatism or openness of these metropolitan magazines and national broadsheets than they do about our project. Our explorations continued, though, and, to some extent, I pursue them still: not now as a movement director, but in my own teaching, research, and professional practice, increasingly internationally. With the growth of practice research, industry/education partnerships, and universities' internationalisation, Letts' dismissive remark now seems totally outdated.

As this was a Platform prompted by and ostensibly about the new production of *Rutherford*, as we called it for short, McIntosh questions what role movement has in the 'more familiar world of *Ghosts* and *Rutherford* [where] you still work with a movement person'. Mitchell responds: 'we were starting to repeat devices, acapella Eastern European music, repeating ourselves, candlelight, earth on the floor [...] I wanted to prove that I could do a show without all of that, just a room, and just the actors in it. That's what led to *Ghosts* and also *Rutherford*. I wanted to work more intimately on the psychology of actors' (*Daily Telegraph*, 1990).

McIntosh raises questions, which this Element will address, of how movement can function for training and as a rehearsal tool for a range of performances, not just plays like *The Dybbuk* or *Live Like Pigs*, where there are specific scripted movement behaviours or sequences such as dances, fights or possession (the latter is at the heart of *The Dybbuk*, as explained in Section 1). To accommodate such texts, our approach became increasingly flexible as it developed, informed by lessons learnt from our first investigation for *Arden*.

As we collaborated more, we observed that the actors were making different choices, that the work was more muscular, and that the physical training and group singing had knit the cast closely together. It discouraged an over-intellectual approach. We became less rigid in our expectations about what was possible in the relatively short rehearsal periods available. We made a further adaptation of increasingly using chi kung (a martial art), stillness-based practices, and breathwork, techniques which I had learnt at university before my immersion in Polish theatre. These approaches, explained in Section 2, were more easily implemented in the British context. They still put the body first, though, rather than beginning from an analytical desk-based focus on readings of the text.

Poland and Movement, Both Near and Far

Listening to the Platform thirty years after it was recorded, two things struck me. Firstly, assumptions and generalisations are made about Eastern Europe, Russia, and Ukraine, which had only recently opened up after the Berlin Wall fell in November 1989, followed by the collapse of the Soviet Union in December 1991. One attendee asks about Mitchell's productions' 'gloom and darkness' and whether this aspect of Eastern Europe informed her directing, which she strongly denied. Public understanding of and contact with those regions is very different today and is certainly much more nuanced, although many prejudices and large knowledge gaps undoubtedly remain.

A second striking factor was the curiosity about the movement, perhaps because movement directors and the processes we followed were then a rarity. Jane Gibson had been Head of Movement at the RNT for ten years (I have been unable to establish the exact dates), but she was probably the only one in the UK then in such a formal institutional position. Movement director and choreographer Struan Leslie corroborates this by stating how unusual it was:

> Katie has always needed to have someone to come and work with her, consistently, and through all her work, as a movement director, connecting the thought to the body [...] regarding my work with her, she has been a trailblazer in that sense. In theatre now there is barely a show that doesn't have a movement director on the team. (*Contemporary Theatre Review*, 2020: 242)

Leslie worked on over thirty productions with Mitchell after our collaboration ended. He does not, however, fully acknowledge my explorations with Mitchell before his engagement in 1995, nor those of Emma Rice, who had performed with Gardzienice before her shift to directing with Kneehigh, The Globe Theatre, and Wise Children, renamed the Emma Rice Company in summer 2025. Rice was movement director for Mitchell on three performances and acted in more, all at a similar period to me. Mitchell's trailblazing had begun five years earlier. Leslie much later became a pioneer himself when, in 2009, he was appointed as the RSC's first Head of Movement. The Platform was exploring uncharted territories regarding both geographical and cultural influence and theatre-making.

As Leslie indicated, Mitchell 'needed' such collaborators: 'I don't work alone. I work with a team of people'. In the Platform, Mitchell explains that she is 'not trained in movement work, but the actor needs to be physically trained in order to work, so then it became obvious that one needed a separate specialist'. She was 'Wanting to do at least 2 hours movement a day, at least 2 hours singing a day' and 'Wanting them [the actors] to work in a more imaginative way in terms of space' (Platform, 1994). Few of our rehearsal periods could accommodate such a daily amount, but in the first week, at least for some of our productions, this was the norm. Occasionally, we had even more all-cast time before the work split into individual or small group calls.

In her book *The Director's Craft* (2009), Mitchell briefly covers the position and responsibilities of the role of movement director in rehearsals and how it relates to the director's work and their authority. She defines three predominantly technical functions of movement work: 'to warm up the actors [...] to prepare the actors' bodies for the specific physical demands of the play [...] and to build up the physical or dance skills used directly in the action' (95–97). On the subject of movement, voice, and text, her book says little other than emphasising the need for the voice to be relaxed and for the director to approach it with great sensitivity, as it can become a sticking point for actors. She also recommends working on movement and voice closely together, with the latter following the former. Mitchell captures aspects of the role succinctly, but in focusing on techniques and skills, she simplifies the possibilities of what movement can do for actors and the role it has in generating the mise en scène and in the overall theatre-making process. This Element advocates for the complexity of movement and its centrality to the actor's work. It also looks closely, in Section 3 mainly, at how movement relates to the voice and textual delivery.

A Polish Tradition

By focusing on a particular strand of the Polish tradition of acting, a key influence on myself and Mitchell, I hope to offer new insights into and alternative narratives of the development of movement directing in the UK. In most existing accounts, recognition of how the body and movement might interact with voice and text is lacking. Jerzy Grotowski was a key authority for me; his approach is documented in *Towards a Poor Theatre* (1968), which has several sections on physical and vocal exercises. The book foregrounds core concepts for the voice and text: the use of resonators; the muscularity of the voice so that it 'surrounds' the spectators; the actor's capacity to open their voice in a released way (linked to the idea of *via negativa*, that is, the removal of psychological and physical blocks and resistance); extraordinary use of the voice so that it goes well beyond daily speech; and total respiration.

In addition, bodywork must always lead, as advocated by Mitchell. For Grotowski, 'My main principle is: Do not think of the vocal instrument itself, do not think of the words, but react – react with the body. The body is the first vibrator and resonator' (Grotowski, 1968: 185). He believed that 'The goal is to find a meeting between the text and the actor' (250). For him, rehearsal and training were not about discovering the author or playwright's intentions but a living connection with the word, in the body. To some extent, this was my aim in rehearsals with Mitchell.

Interestingly, similar criticisms about the use of voice that Mitchell has faced were levelled at Grotowski's performances too. Fowler cites Nick Hytner's 'coming to "dread" her dark and inaudible previews' (Fowler, 2021: 2). Some critics raised concerns about Grotowski's disregard for the text and the performers' mode of textual delivery, which was often incanted or even sung, very fast. Interestingly, some of these did not know Polish, questioning the validity of their views. In her book, Mitchell openly acknowledges problems with audibility, especially in larger auditoria with over 500 seats. Her justification is that this is a side effect of her actors' search for psychological believability. She does recommend collaboration with voice experts, if possible, but this has not always mitigated the problem in production. I will discuss the implications of this in Section 3.

Gardzienice's practice built further on Grotowski's principles, with even greater emphasis on the voice, music, and rhythm: their performances always start from song, with movement growing from it, the musical score preceding and shaping the mise en scène. This approach, which started with Grotowski's Teatr Laboratorium (Laboratory Theatre) and then developed through Gardzienice, has been extended by Polish companies such as Teatr Zar (Wrocław), Teatr Chorea (Lòdż), and Pieśń Kozła (Song of the Goat, formerly Wrocław, now peripatetic). The leaders of these groups all collaborated with Gardzienice in various capacities.

Until very recently, Physical Theatre has not existed as an independent genre in Poland, as it has for decades in the UK, and this is also the case across most of continental Europe. Groups were working in this tradition, such as Henryk Tomaszewski's mime theatre in Wrocław (Wrocławski Teatr Pantomimy im. Henryka Tomaszewskiego), but these were not defined as Physical Theatre. British scholar Jen Harvie attributes this partly to the dominance of text in UK theatre, a feature not shared by many mainland European countries, including Poland (Harvie, 2005: 112–155). In the UK, this led to the establishment of a different kind of body-based or visual theatre, which was not text-centric, as a counterpart to the mainstream. The practice of all these Polish companies can be defined quite simply as acting, rather than according to any specific movement practices or as Physical Theatre. Acting for these groups was, and is, inherently physical, just as it was, and is, extremely vocal and musical, although it has never been called musical theatre either. It is theatre, albeit of a particular kind, even though these groups create performances that share much with dance, at least regarding the performers' physical commitment and their virtuosity and complexity. In these companies, it follows then that there is no separate role of a movement director: the artistic director tends singularly to oversee the creative process and mise en scène, often in close collaboration with the actors.

Although their processes and ours have aspects in common, Mitchell's and my approach to text and rehearsal was much more traditional than that of these Polish companies, even if both began from a similar repertoire of exercises and shared principles related to breath and bodywork. Our practice also took place in a very different context, culture, and structure from that of Grotowski and Gardzienice. Mitchell is an expert at textual analysis and an important advocate for the value of detailed and precise text work in rehearsals. Her initial schooling and experiences as a director began as a student of English and in extracurricular productions at the University of Oxford. We wished to find a meeting ground between her directorial approach, with texts that were usually neither adapted nor cut, and the methods which Mitchell had observed in Central and Eastern Europe and Russia, some of which I was bringing into the rehearsal room. For us, it was less about confrontation with the text, a term Grotowski often used, and more about our wish to make words come alive in new ways by grounding them in the body.

This challenge would be felt most acutely, perhaps unsurprisingly, in our work together on *Henry VI*, as Section 3 will explore. This production exposed one of the main difficulties with the 'marriage' of Polish techniques and British traditions: the use of text. It could be argued that nothing represents the British institution of theatre and its traditional values with textual dominance more than Shakespeare, and none more so than his history plays.

Scholarship and Autoethnography

Movement studies related to theatre and about movement directing specifically comprise a relatively new field. Publications that describe or focus on the role of the movement director have only emerged as recently as 2020 onwards (Tashkiran, 2020, and Flatt, 2022). Numerous texts have examined individual movement practices or tried to define where movement sits in the UK institutionally (Evans, 2009), but none of these have analysed this role. This is not surprising. Mark Evans has argued that 'the current mainstream principles and practices for the movement training of actors remain substantially underresearched' (2009: 3). More recently, Rachel Fensham has suggested that a focus on movement is still an undervalued area: 'In theatre history, while dramatic theories shaped the study of literary genres such as tragedy and comedy, and psychological theories have examined acting, authenticity and the study of emotion in theatre, there is unfortunately no equivalent body of writings on movement for theatre' (Fensham, 2021: 3). There are many texts on individual practitioners but few authoritative overviews, and none with the angle proposed here that will reflect on extensive personal professional experience. Fensham analyses case studies from theatre, dance, and performance/live art, to understand 'how we define movement in performance' (2021). Her book is written from the perspective of a critical spectator, very different from this project with its self-reflexive and exclusively theatre-focused approach.

British scholarship on movement directing draws mainly from either the French tradition of physical work or from dance and is often in the form of handbooks or teaching manuals. Tashkiran's 2020 book and Evans' two works are informed predominantly by Jacques Lecoq's practice, with whom they both trained. Evans' 2009 text largely focuses on British institutional histories and the dynamics in which training happens, as well as the influence of key figures on this (Frederick Alexander, Jacques Copeau, Rudolf von Laban, Jacques Lecoq). His more recent text (2019) analyses the training of actors and the development of skills across different forms, teachers/trainers and companies, mainly in the UK, including circus, Frantic Assembly, and Lecoq. Tashkiran's edited collection of interviews with movement directors focuses on professional practice and craft, only briefly contextualising and thematising the range of movement directing it presents. Like Green and Ewan (2015), Flatt's 2022 book and practice both evolved out of dance; for Flatt, choreography is a key aspect of movement.

Few works make much, if any, reference to Polish or Eastern European traditions of acting and movement, though Evans' later work does pay it some attention, as does Fensham with her examination of Grotowski's performance of *The Constant Prince* (1965). This is a significant gap, especially when two things are considered: Polish theatre's extensive influence on British theatre and performance, notably Physical Theatre, and its strong explorations of voice training and vocal performance. The latter is a dimension that most movement books ignore.

An absence has also been noted regarding Mitchell's work. In the introduction to the *Contemporary Theatre Review* special issue on Mitchell, the editors observed that in my short contribution, I write about 'a phase of Mitchell's work that has received almost no scholarly attention, and it is our hope that his recollections will ignite interest in it' (Cornford and Svich, 2020: 149). Duška Radosavljević has an interview with Leslie in the same issue, which is 'concerned with surfacing and documenting an otherwise invisible aspect of Katie Mitchell's oeuvre as a director' (238), including 'her engagement with choreography and movement in rehearsal, and the role of a movement director in facilitating it' (149). As mentioned earlier, this only starts from 1995, but it also has a different emphasis from mine. Leslie is dance-trained, explaining a further distinction between our approaches. I would never describe my work as choreography, though interestingly, the summative production cast and crew lists compiled by *Theatre Record* in their online archive frequently and erroneously label me as the Choreographer. This indicates the widespread lack of understanding about the role. Leslie charts the shift that came about in Mitchell's practice with his involvement, from movement to movement plus choreography.

Evans states that having to 'sometimes write [on the body] from a personal perspective' is 'contrary to academic convention' (2019: 1). This is surprising considering the decades of practice research in the UK and related writings. Indeed, self-reflexive practice research methods and participant observation are well established (see, for example, Kershaw and Nicholson, 2011, especially Pitches et al.'s Chapter 6: Performer Training: Researching Practice in the Theatre Laboratory). Using their terminology, in this Element I will combine historical documentary records of all kinds (textual, audio, and audio-visual) with my own reflective and critical writing. This Element champions an autoethnographic approach, arguing that this gives empirically grounded insights and that personal engagement and lived experience can add vital depth and understanding. Such methods, discussed by Tinius (2024) and Denzin (2013) among many others, are now very familiar, even if they do not come without their own complexities and problems.

As I am aware of the pitfalls of subjective analysis and the biases this can introduce (Chang, 2016), I have triangulated my reflections from my notebooks with others' perspectives and writings, including theatre reviews, interviews, and commentaries, as well as key texts such as Fowler's (2021) and the *Contemporary Theatre Review* on Mitchell (2020). Other scholarship on Mitchell's work, including her excellent authored book from 2009, has further helped contextualise my reflections. Reading reviews has given me insights from objective accounts about the contribution movement made to the performances. They balance my notes, which are mainly about input, the process followed, and our intentions, assessing these against external evaluation of the results and the performances. In considering critics' reviews, I have not been interested in their overall evaluation of a production's success, but in how they have documented or reflected on aspects that might pertain to my contribution as movement director. I have tried to interpret fairly their perspectives in relation to the role I played.

I have drawn on film documentation of performances where available in archives, but there are problems with looking back so far in time. The historical distance has the benefit that my research has not been impeded by temporal proximity to the events and processes explored. I can detach myself from the process's emotional intensity. On the downside, *Rutherford and Son* was presented before the RNT filmed all its performances, and no video record exists. Even where recordings do exist and are available for scrutiny, they are often poorly documented on VHS with single cameras located behind the audience and with weak audio. The video of *The Dybbuk*, housed in the Shakespeare Birthplace Trust Archive in Stratford-upon-Avon, UK, is very dark, as is the recording of *The Machine Wreckers* (RNT Archive). Much of Mitchell's early work used low lighting and candles, none more so than *The Dybbuk*'s Act One. Watching the *Dybbuk* film helped me as an aide memoire, but it was only useful because of my involvement in the project. To those without such experience, it will serve a minimal purpose. Performance documentation has come a long way since, as the success of online platforms like Digital Theatre+ or DramaOnline attests, although we still need to improve the filming of process, as my article on this topic argues (Allain, 2023).

This Element is in three Sections. Section 1 explores issues of representation and how movement helps performers become others by enacting cultural and social differences. It considers what responsibilities come with such representations. Section 2 examines how movement can be utilised in rehearsals to create an ensemble and diverse worlds on stage across a range of texts and genres, as well as for character development and acting. A common aspect across Sections 1 and 2 is how movement practices can help contribute to the spatial aspects of a performance. Section 3 examines movement as a creative element within text-based performances, with specific reference to text and vocal delivery and musical work. An unusual addition that is discussed in this section with reference to two early modern case studies is how movement can help with killing and dying on stage.

1 Enacting Cultural Difference

This section focuses on two productions, *The Dybbuk* (RSC, 1992) and, more briefly, *Live Like Pigs* (Royal Court Theatre Upstairs, 1991). Both plays required the casts to depict unusual worlds and characters. This unfamiliarity was complex and multiple, including historical, cultural, and, in the first case, geographical distance, as well as class and religious otherness, as will be explained. These applied to each actor or production team member differently, according to their backgrounds and lived experiences. My movement practice was crucial in both productions to help the cast inhabit these worlds, but also to enact specific, textually prescribed moments of action.

The Dybbuk, or Between Two Worlds (1913–16)

If you read the cast list of Sh. An-sky's play, you might consider it a movement director's dream: a hunchback, a blind old woman, a poor man on crutches, and an old limping woman.[1] These are some of the poor invited to the wedding at the heart of the play, following the Jewish custom of giving food to the needy at such events. Beyond this, the *dramatis personae* yields few hints of what other riches the play has. As an ethnographically grounded recreation of a story about an Orthodox Jewish community in Ukraine before the First World War, with its

---

[1] All character names are taken from the prompt copy for our production (*The Dybbuk*, 1992), available in the RSC archive. Most play text citations are also from this source, though I sometimes reference the Joseph C. Landis 1966 edition in which there are fuller stage directions. Names in citations have not been altered, and in some reviews of our production, alternative spellings have been used.

traditions, religious practices, and beliefs, the play offers a great deal. Beyond the need to represent the poor accurately and respectfully, the question of how best to depict this world on stage was daunting. Director Katie Mitchell and I faced numerous challenges in the production, on which I worked as movement director.

The Dybbuk, as it is usually known for short, captures with great accuracy a now-disappeared community on the verge of extinction, about to face the horrors of the First World War. It revolves around the Jewish belief that a spirit from a dead body that is in limbo can enter another person. One of the reasons for the text's verisimilitude is that An-sky, as he liked to be known (his real name was Shloyme Zanvl Rappoport), had himself conducted fieldwork across the Pale of Settlement to such communities which he depicts in the play.

The location for the play is a shtetl in Central and Eastern Europe, where a young woman, Leye, is to be married off to a rich suitor by her wealthy father, Reb Sender. Her preferred suitor, Khonen, has been dabbling in the Kabbalah, a mystical and esoteric Jewish practice and philosophy, exploring how to ensure that she will marry him instead. Dismayed at the end of Act One to hear of her planned betrothal, he collapses and dies in the synagogue.

In Act Two, Leye is about to be married. There is a community wedding dance and feast during which she suddenly becomes possessed after visiting Khonen's grave. A pact (explained shortly) and Khonen's ardour have led to his soul becoming so restless that it returns to earth to inhabit Leye as a 'clinging demon', a dybbuk (Freedman, 2019). In Act Three, there is an attempt to dispel the dybbuk from her, but to no avail. Rabbi Azriel is therefore called to conduct a formal exorcism. On arriving, Reb Azriel says how Reb Nissen, Khonen's father, visited him in a dream and explained the pact that Sender and he had when they were young men, agreeing to marry their children. Nissen accuses Sender of being responsible for his son's death. Act Four includes a litigation to establish Sender's culpability and then the exorcism. The dybbuk is forced out, but only at the expense of Leye, who dies and joins Khonen. A mysterious Messenger, a narrator/observer figure, comments on and predicts certain events and mediates between the audience and the play.

I will describe and analyse some of the processes we undertook to create the religious rituals and practices of this community, with its very specific culture, as well as to depict the possession at the play's core. This begs questions about acting, representation, and cultural appropriation. Many critics applauded our efforts, with Paul Taylor from the *Independent* observing that 'Her wonderfully absorbing account of *The Dybbuk*, just opened at The Pit, illustrates again her talent for imparting the sense of a close community, drawing you this time into a Hasidic Jewish enclave in turn-of-the-century Eastern Europe' (*Independent*,

1992). I will also examine what being a movement director for this production involved, a role that was then quite rare.

I will consider selected examples from the production history of the play and film versions to ground my personal experience and autoethnographic reflections in a broader context. Western film history offers us a much better-known version of a similar Christian concept in *The Exorcist* (1973). The film has lost little of its power over time: human possession is something that fascinates us and transcends cultures. In it, the body possessed is that of an American child, 12-year-old Regan, played by 14-year-old Linda Blair. *The Dybbuk* also features a young woman being possessed, Leye, who is probably not much more than a child, although her age is never specified. In cinema, possession can be portrayed through editing, make-up, costume changes, and, increasingly today, CGI and many other technological processes. Theatre's inherent liveness makes this a much greater challenge.

Although not Jewish, Mitchell was curious about how to engage artistically with what is undoubtedly one of the worst atrocities of the twentieth century. When asked at the National Theatre Platform what influenced her choice of plays, Mitchell responded that '[*The*] *Dybbuk* was a fascination with trying to understand the Holocaust, especially in a climate of growing nationalism' (Platform, 1994). An earlier interview explained more:

> 'Before I directed "The Dybbuk" in 1991 [sic], I followed (playwright Solomon) An-sky's footprints into the Ukraine', Mitchell says, sitting at the head of a large table in the Cerritos Performing Arts Center conference room. 'The play says nothing of the Holocaust, but it foretold the Holocaust. Yet it remained this most beautiful love story, didn't it? Beautiful and sensual and deeply private'. (Christon, 1994)

Historian Michael C. Steinlauf's view of the play is that 'For Jews, that is, the play functioned as a powerful spectacle of national affirmation – even as it stealthily undermined all affirmation. The carefully constructed Hasidic milieu, along with the channelling of the premodern folklore of demonic possession, became central elements of nearly all subsequent productions of the play, both before and after the Holocaust' (in Abramowicz et al., 2017: 27). None of our core creative team members were Jewish, so we immersed ourselves in extensive research into Jewish culture and history, rituals, and beliefs before rehearsals.

Mitchell is renowned for her meticulous preparation, which often includes fieldwork or site visits, this time to Ukraine from 16 to 26 April 1992. The community that An-sky presents and many like it were largely decimated in the Second World War. Our aim was not to immerse ourselves in a still extant world, as an anthropologist might. Instead, we sought indirect knowledge and inspiration, wanting to understand better the context from which such a work arose and where the community lived, as well as find expertise beyond that available in London and the UK.

To us young British artists, the strangeness and otherness of Ukraine then, which had only recently become independent after the 1991 collapse of the Soviet Union and was perhaps itself 'Between two worlds', helped us to understand *The Dybbuk*'s context. It fed into the play. Although much of this inspiration was indirect in terms of it being another world and time, the largely unchanged climate and rural landscapes impacted our process directly, with the cold and mud that pervades in shtetls, as just one example. How to walk in thick mud became a key movement task in early rehearsals.

Benjamin Fowler discusses our fieldwork. He goes on to cite Paul Taylor's view that

> the production never gives the impression of simply unpacking in public its ethnic souvenirs. The play envisages a spooked world of swaying Talmudic scholars, anxiously arranged marriages, superstitious folk tales, and rabbinical trials in which the dead can be summoned up as witnesses, but Mitchell's version has a fully inhabited feel. (in Fowler, 2021: 52)

Fowler notes that such an approach would 'now be likely to raise suspicions of cultural appropriation and anthropological tourism' (Fowler, 2021: 52). He argues that 'Mitchell's anthropological phase involved studying behaviour without consciously foregrounding the politics of perspectival dynamics in the art she was making, as would later become her interest' (Fowler, 2021: 52). There is an implied criticism here that some of her early work, including *The Dybbuk*, was decontextualised and apolitical. I would argue that a performance that meticulously recreates a disappeared world of a Jewish community in a venue just four miles away from Stamford Green, where the displaced Hasidic community still thrives, could be considered a very strong political and cultural statement. The fact that, at the time of writing, the full-scale war in Ukraine has entered its fourth year, with Russia attempting to destroy Ukrainian society and culture, shows how much cultural acts can have political implications.

It is worth briefly considering some notable productions to contextualise ours. In the UK, Julia Pascal directed a version in the same year as our RSC production. Coincidentally, in January 1992, Peter Brook's actor Bruce Myers also devised and performed a two-hander in the UK, which later toured internationally. The play has been staged frequently in North America and Poland; however, many of these performances have been exploratory responses to the text or adaptations, including the British ones. My interest here is more in how one might represent the play on stage in its entirety, rather than using it as a springboard. This aligns with Polish film director Agnieszka Holland's ambition for her 1999 TVP (Polish Television) version: 'Usually when Polish directors tackle Jewish subjects, I feel a kind of irritation because it's like a fairy tale. But I wanted to show Jewish life in a very realistic way. Realism establishes a direct emotional connection between the characters and the audience, so that even if you have no Jewish background, you can relate' (Pfefferman, 2003). Such realism is arguably easier to create on film.

Our production was presented in The Pit in the Barbican Centre, London, a small, flexible studio theatre with 164 seats. It is a high-profile venue, especially as it was the Royal Shakespeare Company's metropolitan base before all operations were moved back to Stratford-upon-Avon. The play has many challenges, but having the substantial resources and technical know-how of the RSC behind us made our task easier and allowed an unusually long rehearsal period. The production attracted some interest at the time, though it is surprising what a small footprint it has today, especially given Mitchell's current international profile. It does not merit a single page in Fowler's 253-page book on Mitchell (2021), although he does write at length about her 'anthropological phase' overall.

Mitchell was still very much cutting her teeth as a director, though she was beginning to establish a reputation, mostly in the UK. An American article describes how she was perceived by the then-director of the RSC:

> When she joined the RSC as assistant director, Adrian Noble saw a young woman 'full of vim and ideas, and passionate about how theater and society interface. She's a curious mix of anthropologist and artist. When she did "The Dybbuk" for us, she conducted such an extraordinary eight- to 10-week rehearsal that by the end she transformed the company into Ukrainian Jews. And she's not Jewish. She's not bound by social realism. She's got theatrical poetry'. (Christon, 1994)

Noble's comments are interesting. *The Dybbuk* was an unusual choice for the RSC, an expensive risk with a cast of twenty-four and long rehearsals, and a sign of the faith with which Mitchell was then entrusted. Although it was presented in its more experimental space, The Pit, the play sits anomalously in the RSC's repertoire. However, once the piece was facing the public, albeit in a more protected mode in previews with cheaper tickets before the Press Night and actual run, the institution seems to have gotten cold feet. Noble visited the first preview, as production notes contained in the RSC Archive attest, and tried swiftly to redirect aspects. He wanted to brighten the lighting and increase the volume of some lines. I remember it well. It was a bruising experience, especially for Mitchell. Noble's concerns were felt more acutely because his wife, Joanne Pearce, was playing Leye.

Noble was possibly wrestling with trying to understand the balance between Mitchell's realism and her 'theatrical poetry'. Returning to Holland's comments, productions usually either face into the play text's realist challenge or experiment or adapt, although these are not mutually exclusive. The kind of verisimilitude Mitchell chose has not, throughout history, appealed to all commentators: 'these elite audiences [in the Russian Empire] insisted that the play was too literary and folkloric for the stage' (Caplan and Moss, 2023: 6). Mitchell herself later reflected critically on the performance, stating that 'The production was a bit museumy' (Platform, 1994).

Questions and reservations aside, our task was to create a credible recreation of the life of the Hasidic community on which the play is based. Much of this fell to my role in terms of helping the cast to embody this culture. In addition, the transformation and possession of Leye had to be believable enough for two distinct groups: the play's community must understand that Khonen has entered Leye's body and speaks through her and needs to be exorcised, and the audience must believe in the possession and its threat to Leye. The fact that she tragically dies at the end of the play reinforces the need to make it serious and believable: this loss is the individual tragedy at the text's heart, a symbolic representation of the fate that the entire Jewish community was later to face en masse.

There are few clues in the text about how to play the possession, even though it is a key element of the drama. We learn little through how others respond to or describe the situation: she is called 'mad' (*The Dybbuk*, 1992: 27), but not much is concretely indicated other than great fear during the exorcism in particular. Regarding stage directions, there is minimal information. Initially, Leye 'tears herself away, runs to [the] little grave, spreads out her arms . . . . She falls'. This is just before and part of the beginning of her actual possession at the very end of Act Two (26). In Act Three, 'She stops stubbornly at the threshold and doesn't want to enter . . . She sits down obediently. Suddenly she jumps up and screams not with her own voice . . . She wants to run out' (14–15). 'Sender and Frade try to take Leye out . . . Frade manages to take Leye out' (20). Textual information relates mostly to directional movement on stage and entrances and exits, rather than how An-sky envisaged the possession being enacted.

As the story unfolds, there are a few more indicators in Act Four when the exorcism is described in more detail as she 'jerks out of her seat, throws herself about' (35) and then utters: 'I can struggle . . . no more' (36). This is as much as the playwright gives us in stage directions, though Leye's reflection on what is happening to her also conveys a vivid image of the effects of the exorcism: 'I am torn by terrible angels . . . As long as I have strength, I will fight' (35). With a 'violent shudder', she (or rather Khonen through Leye) asks for Kaddish, the prayer for the dead, to be spoken or sung (38). Given An-sky's interest in and experience of ethnography, it must be assumed that he took information about possession from in-the-field sources as well as literature that was then available.

We discovered several descriptions of how dybbuks enter the body. Just as the restless spirit can only enter through an extremity or 'hole', including under a fingernail, so 'The spirit was to leave the body only between the big toe and its nail; any other exit route might cause permanent damage to the possessed person' (Freedman, 2019). It could also leave through the rectum or vagina, reinforcing the sexual aspect of such possessions. According to Jewish folklore, dybbuks usually, though not exclusively, took control of women and were also most often men. In *The Exorcist*, Regan masturbates violently with a crucifix in a shocking scene. The widespread interest in possession might be linked to its inherent violence and sexual fantasising. We discussed this in rehearsal, avoiding any overt sexualisation as in *The Exorcist*, while not completely ignoring this aspect. She wets herself at one point, and some of Leye's vocalisations hinted at sexual sounds.

A dybbuk possession often has a strong vocal dimension. Once inside the body, the spirit's voice dominates and speaks through its host. The initial vocal transformation in Leye is depicted as follows: 'She looks around wildly and screams, not with her own voice, with the voice of a man' (*The Dybbuk*, 1992: 26). In the stage directions, her voice shifts from 'Softly' to 'Shouting' to 'trembling' within a couple of minutes. At one point, she 'awakens, in her own voice' (Landis, 1966: 56). When she speaks when possessed, she often addresses herself, making it clear that Khonen is talking through her. Act Two ends with the possession being confirmed by the enigmatic Messenger's unambiguous closing words, in Yiddish, then English in our version: 'In der kalle iz arayn a dybbuk, The bride has been entered by a dybbuk' (*The Dybbuk*, 1992: 27). This was followed by 'Great confusion'.

Taylor commented on this vocal aspect, noting how it was so intrinsically connected to her physicality: 'Pearce's performance pre-empts any titters in the episodes of possession too. When Khonen's voice, in a brain-damaged slur, prises itself through, she trails round a crippled-looking foot or jerks her throat forward as if she has been inhabited by a spirit that can only take up residence in one bit of her at a time' (*Independent*, 1992). Such an enactment was mostly achieved through substantial one-to-one work that I conducted with Pearce. The vocal 'illusion', if we may call it that, was helped by the fact that Pearce has a naturally low, gravelly voice; although we also needed to portray the difference between Leye before and after her possession. Her deep voice was useful not so much because it sounded masculine and could therefore represent the possessing dybbuk, but because it was already connected to and came from deep inside her body, a 'supported' voice as it is called in training. Her strong chest voice, connected to her deep breathing and active diaphragm, provided a good technical starting point for such exploratory work.

We eschewed all recorded effects to enhance the voice, though other productions and films have deployed technology. Sidney Lumet's 1960 film, described as a new adaptation, uses voice in a very different way from ours, as film can easily do. When her possession is revealed, Khonen's voice overlays hers, though louder, as they speak simultaneously. Lumet later uses another kind of voiceover. With piano music in the background and the sound of Nissen's heartbeat, the camera focuses on faces, including the Rabbi's as well as that of Reb Sender, who turns his face slowly from side to side. At this point, we hear the voice of Khonen's father, Nissen, in a flashback that reveals their pact.

The double-voiced possession is also deployed later in the film. Leye faints in her father's arms as soon as she enters the synagogue and is carried by her father to a table. In her own voice, she speaks simultaneously the same words as Khonen, though his dominate. As she has fainted, it is only his soul and voice that make her 'alive'. When he has departed from her, she stands like a rag doll and does a convulsive dance which turns into balletic twirling. The dance becomes more representational as she attempts to fly, mimed gesturally by her waving her arms and hands.

So little is textually prescribed, especially in our 1992 rehearsal copy, meaning that the possession can be enacted in multiple ways: through suggestive or abstract means, as in Lumet's version; through dance, music, or other approaches (multimedia or animation possibilities spring to mind today); or through realist enactment, such as we attempted. In the play's most famous rendition by the Habima Theatre in Moscow in 1922, director Evgeny Vakhtangov made a clear stylistic choice, as Russian theatre specialist Vera Gottlieb recounts:

> a 'grotesque folklore' – and in turning its back on naturalism, it became a theatre free of convention in which lighting, music, ritual, mystery, were all 'natural' ingredients of the production, a production often described as 'Expressionist'. Influencing Vakhtangov was also the art of Goya, of Daumier – and Chagall. By utilising the 'verisimilitude' of ritual and folklore, it enabled the staging of subjective perceptions, leading to distorted angles, nightmarish contrast between light and dark, mass scenes in which the movement and action were choreographed by Vakhtangov as a musical score of gesture. (Gottlieb, 2005)

We can get some indication of what the piece might have looked like from 'The Dance of Death', a section of the celebrated 1937 film version of the play directed by Michał Waszyński. This draws on Vakhtangov's production, with a large cast of thirty-one (see the extract in Kafrissen, 2022). Black and white stills, widely available online, also indicate the piece's aesthetics. Gestures were exaggerated, actors wore distorting make-up, and stage furniture had unusual angles. Musicality and rhythm were foregrounded, especially in the wedding dance (a clip was shown in the exhibition *The Dybbuk: Phantom of the Lost World*, 2024–2025). In a *New York Times* review, J. Brooks Atkinson describes how 'When all these separate parts are pulled together in a symmetrical performance, the effect is astonishing – as unreal as the mystical legend of the play, as profound in its searching of the emotions, supple, resilient and varied' (Atkinson, 1926). We studied such sources, but this approach could not have been further from our quest for verisimilitude.

Avia Moore's more recent 2011 all-female-identifying production in Montreal precluded any sexual binaries in the possession, an attempt to reclaim agency for Leye. Moore even left it ambiguous whether she was possessed or was just performing the possession. With a cast of five women and much doubling of roles, it departed a long way from the source. Her treatment aligns with Polish scholar Agnieszka Legutko's view of the play, whom Moore cites as a key influence:

> An-sky's *The Dybbuk* revolutionized the dybbuk possession trope by transforming it into a modernist artistic device, thus departing from its traditional use as a cautionary tale. Reading the play through the lenses of Judith Butler's theory of gender as a performed cultural construct, one may posit that An-sky depicts possession as a 'performance act' staged by the female protagonist in order to challenge the power dynamic in society and take control over her own life. (Legutko in Abramowicz et al., 2017: 121)

Given the extent of its departure from the original, this production is of less interest here, though it joins a catalogue of numerous versions and adaptations, many of them referenced or described in *The Dybbuk Century* (2023). Even more extreme was Krzysztof Warlikowski's *Dybbuk*, which 'broke entirely with the assumptions of all previous productions, both Yiddish and Polish. First staged in 2003, Warlikowski's *Dybbuk* eliminated all traces of feel-good folklore from the stage, and refused its audience any sort of resolution' (Steinlauf in Abramowicz et al., 2017: 29). This is one of many Polish versions examined in that collection, with chapters in both English and Polish.

I mention these performances to reveal the range of responses to and adaptations of the text, most of which depart drastically from our approach. Interestingly, *The Dybbuk Century* dedicates a whole chapter to Moore's production, by Moore herself, but it does not even mention our RSC production.

This may in part be because of its dominant focus on North American performances, but it does confirm how our production has passed into relative obscurity. This is surprising considering that the RSC is a major international institution.

Acting, Possession, Realism

There are many ways of approaching the text, of adapting and cutting or using it as a launchpad. Even if one is 'faithful' to the extent of presenting the text in its entirety, many choices remain. Schwartz's 1921 New York version 'chose a large-scale ethnographic show aimed to depict the life of an ancestral generation', with a cast of sixty (Abramowicz et al., 2017: 160). Actress Celia Adler writes of her experience playing the character: 'the role of Leah, especially the scenes where she spoke in Khonon's voice, was exhausting, so much so that on one occasion she actually fainted on stage' (Abramowicz et al., 2017: 161).

Reviewer 'Abraham Koralnik was particularly blatant in voicing his opinion: 'in order to create a cabbalist or a dybbuk one must, yes, must not be an actor. You cannot act Kabbala. Torah was not intended for the theater' (Abramowicz et al., 2017: 162). This extreme view denies the potential of theatre to create other worlds, but it does indicate the difficulty it can entail. One of the stage manager's nightly reports for our production, which are all available in the RSC archive, hints at the complex interconnections between stage reality and real life, especially in work striving for veracity, like ours. One audience member was upset to see scraps of the Torah on stage when some of its pages were ripped up. He wrote a letter to the RSC to request permission to collect and take them away to dispose of them ritually in an appropriate manner, which was honoured. For some people, what happens on stage is not separate from their daily lives.

Paul Taylor gives a slightly flippant account of Mitchell's early work, reflecting on her realism:

> One of Mitchell's key virtues as a director, though, is her ability to think and feel her way into alien cultures, value systems and social atmosphere. She confesses herself a 'closet anthropologist', for whom being given the excuse to investigate ways of life far removed from her own is a major attraction of directing. For her lauded 1992 version of the classic Yiddish play *The Dybbuk*, she went walkabout in the Ukraine, talking to Jewish survivors about their memories of life in the shtetls and recording everything from peasants to birdsong. (*Independent*, 1994)

After this mention of the fieldwork research in Ukraine, he immediately segues into Norway, without clarifying that this was research for her *Ghosts* (1993), on which I also worked as movement director (see Section 2). Yet the impression he gives of the major thrust of her work at that time is clear: its anthropologically based verisimilitude. This approach permeated much of our work together. Later, with *The Waves* (2006) especially, Mitchell moved away from live voice and music. Instead, she chose to create atmospheres and worlds by embracing the possibilities of technology, her 'live cinema'. This period has been widely documented and analysed, including in the 2020 *Contemporary Theatre Review* special issue on Mitchell and in Fowler's two books.

As Taylor observed, the play is striking for the way that it explicitly explores the actor's transformation on stage, showing a woman's body occupied by a man. Few traditional acting models easily accommodate such a process. What is required is very different from, for example, the comedy, exaggerated drag or cross-dressing of popular performance forms like pantomime. The mythical possession also pushes the limits of the audience's suspension of disbelief. Probably very few of us have witnessed a possession, even though detailed descriptions of them abound, many in folklore.

Sheridan Morley was damning, describing the evening as 'very boring' (*Herald Tribune*, 1992). Ian Shuttleworth was critical and disbelieving:

> The performances, too, are studied rather than felt: John Shrapnel's exorcist is a picture of grave authority, Rob Edwards' Messenger one of oracular mystery, but they remain pictures rather than incarnations. Most tellingly, throughout the possession of Leye by the spirit of her suitor Khonen, Joanne Pearce never seems to abandon control; she writhes, vomits blood and pisses herself, but the alienness of movement first unloosed on a stage by David Byrne (I'm serious here) is wholly absent from Leye. (*City Limits*, 1992)

Shuttleworth misses the point that in a dybbuk possession, the departed character's soul and its partial earthly manifestation appear only through their struggle with the still very present host body. The play's drama lies in this conflict and tension, a possession so strong that it eventually kills Leye. She can only 'abandon control' when dead. Her departure comes in the very final moments of the play as she describes the threshold of her passing: 'A great light flows all around. I am bound to you, for all eternity, my beloved.... together we fly higher and higher and higher' (*The Dybbuk*, 1992: 44). The dybbuk itself might be fictional, solely within the 'world of the play' as Mitchell likes to describe it (see Section 2), but her possession and subsequent death must be believable. If not, the audience will care little about the tragic fate of this young woman and her admirer, Khonen. This was an important consideration for our interpretation, although it was not a prerequisite for most of the adaptations described here.

The final scene, when Leye dies and 'joins' Khonen, has been enacted in many ways. At the end of Polish director Maja Kleczewska's 2015 production for Warsaw's Jewish Theatre, the couple lie together on the floor, tightly bound to each other in a playful union (a clip was shown in the Paris exhibition). He is lying face down with her on his back, both with outspread arms as they revolve slowly on the floor. Both wear torn sweaters with lateral slits in them, her hands inserted through one tear so that their arms become one.

Our ending also used conjoined movement and went beyond realism in a moment reminiscent of a sequence of Gardzienice's *Carmina Burana* (1990). Tristan and Isolde, on whose story that performance is based, enact a lyrical, semi-acrobatic duet to a male, choral Georgian song, which they sing while moving, their bodies entwined with simple lifts and holds. In our production, Khonen enters and stands next to Leye in a loose white robe that recalls her white wedding dress. A UV light picks them both out in the darkness. She jumps onto his thighs before standing up and leaning out from both his legs in a balance which I have named 'the Titanic', reminiscent as it is of the moment when Kate Winslet leans forward, supported by Leonardo DiCaprio at the bow of the fateful ship (see 'Acrobatics' in Allain and Camilleri, 2018). Leye speaks the text cited earlier about going higher and higher, accompanied by the fleeting, prerecorded sound effect of dove wings fluttering as they fly away. She then falls gently and safely from his thighs to the floor, after which he holds up one of her arms before letting it go. It drops, a dead weight. She has passed.

This sequence is accompanied by a small ash drop from above and the mournful singing of the Kaddish, sung live and solo by the production's musical director and actor-musician Ben Livingstone. The whole sequence lasts just a couple of minutes, but echoes Gardzienice's approach to layering, one element overlaid onto another to create semantic and sensory depth. It is a powerful conclusion to the play and a symbolic moment which, through the ash drop, speaks to the awful mass murder of Jews in twentieth-century Europe.

Other movements were also inspired by Gardzienice, some of whose exercises were themselves lifted from Jewish culture, though not from a still extant local practice. Rather, they arise from the fact that pre-World War Two, the region where they are based was home to a very large Jewish community. Tangible elements of this existed when I lived in the village in the early 1990s, such as a Jewish headstone that had been turned, sacrilegiously, into a grinding stone. One example of this influence on us was spinning on the spot with outspread arms, a form of Hasidic prayer and celebration, which Gardzienice used in their Gatherings (see Allain, 1997: 31–44 and for an image, Figure 7, np). Leye spins at the start of the wedding dance, holding a scarf in both hands to emphasise the swirling movement. Later, a beggar also spins. Leye's twirling is then extended when she is lifted to sit on the shoulders of one of the beggars, who turns around, albeit more slowly.

The lift anticipates her 'flight' upwards at the end of the play. It is part of a long wedding dance sequence that in the text is initially simply denoted by the stage direction 'She is dancing with poor old women, one after another' (Act Two, Scene Five). The text then includes various lines from the beggars and others about the ongoing dance. This dance sequence was created through improvisations, which sometimes incorporated elements from our Gardzienice-inspired training, such as lifts, simple balances, and spinning. The wedding dance developed from the men doing slow, strong stepping into a much more frenzied conclusion, with three poor people dancing around. Mostly, the men danced separately from the women, as was then the custom. Details were added once the form was established, such as a beggar pawing at Leye's dress. She eventually emerges from a near trance, rather disturbed, recalling 'their arms', as though waking from a bad dream.

Technical aspects of Jewish wedding dances were introduced by visiting expert Shlomo Mamam, an Israeli dancer, in a dedicated movement session. Dances in Norman Jewison's film *Fiddler on the Roof* (1971) were also a useful stimulus. These were both helpful, but the final shape of the wedding dance and its atmosphere, as well as other dances in the text, were created largely through my training exercises and subsequent improvisations. This includes the ecstatic circle dance of the 'Batlans', the unemployed Jewish men, in the synagogue at the end of Act One. With their arms around each other's shoulders, this transforms into a 'happy dance' (np). The RSC archive has a handwritten note by Mitchell on the draft production programme about needing to add the Gardzienice Theatre Association to the acknowledgements, recognising their vital influence.

In terms of the possession, part of the work I led with Pearce one-to-one involved helping her release tension in specific body parts, especially her arms, to show looseness and to give an impression of paralysis or uselessness. She did complex, imaginative tasks. We worked on her appearing to 'be moved' rather than moving according to her own volition. She mirrored me and then resisted mirroring. Her hands wandered of their own accord, and she watched them, puzzled.

We asked questions that we explored practically: what if she lacked any sense of touch? Could she be like a rag doll, as if propped up by nothing more than Khonen's presence? We explored looking but not seeing and letting the jaw fall slack so that the voice emerged from within, as if bypassing the vocal cords and mouth, a kind of ventriloquism. We asked how she might surprise herself physically, if indeed it is possible when the person being surprised is doing the surprising. We played with stillness and impulses, asking where the centre is. We looked at tics and Tourette's, violent jerks and fast responses, self-mutilation, and extraordinary strength. Might she imitate people around her, accurately? Might she be attracted to spinning objects? Taylor recognised the value of our efforts:

> Joanne Pearce brings a haunting quality of loneliness to the role. The conflict between her deep spiritual need for reunion with Khonen and the impending arranged marriage to a man she has never seen is brought out thrillingly when the sudden clashing sounds of a merry, distant wedding band startle Leye from preoccupied quietness into the panic-stricken disarray of a cornered animal. (*Independent*, 1992)

We charted where the dybbuk enters and departs the body and wondered how to show its progression inside. Isolation exercises, drawn from mime and then developed by Grotowski, which isolate specific areas of the body, such as the chest or a wrist, allowed Pearce to have a clear sense of where the dybbuk was inside her at any time. This was informed by written accounts of it moving around the body under the skin like a ball, visible even to an observer, movements she had to imagine. This precise progression would then be interrupted by total physical shaking and trembling, as Leye momentarily lost control and was completely overcome by the alien presence.

I led impulse work with the cast. At the start of the wedding, Leye is brought in by two people who hold and try to contain her when she is first possessed. She writhes in their grip, moving from the pelvic area, her head and upper body loose. This sequence is akin to a Gardzienice exercise, which I often use for actors, as it especially helps them find a connection between breath, voice, and the diaphragm. One person stands still with two others on either side holding them loosely by the hands. The central figure starts to move from the pelvis, looking to find strong, dynamic, but released movement from their centre. With the legs grounded and a relaxed upper body, the sensation of freedom felt when moving vigorously while being gently held and supported by two others is psychologically and vocally liberating (See 'Text Work' in Allain and Camilleri, 2018). It was a perfect choice for the initial possession, showing the ambiguity that her body was not her own, allowing her to writhe as she still somehow managed to retain some control. She then collapsed to the floor, twisting as Khonen's deep voice emanated from her belly. Technically, we explored ways of falling to make the floor 'soft' and safe, to help her cope with abrupt falls and being dropped. Releasing the outbreath on a downward movement helped relax the body and soften the impact.

On the first day of rehearsal, we learnt a chi kung sequence, a Chinese martial art which tries to release energy blockages in the joints and unify movement with the breath (see Allain, 1994, and Section 2). We did stretches from shiatsu (Japanese acupressure), warmed each other up by shaking another's limbs, and did rhythmical choral work, such as moving and stopping together. Emulating the Hasidim, we opened our bodies up to the heavens with joy. We then read the play twice together. On day two, I led a simple circle social dance with forward and backwards stepping, which evolved into spontaneous dancing, informed by a sense of being possessed by a fear of holy things. On day three, while moving around the room, we physically explored the behavioural rules for women, such as not looking at each other and not being able to touch (the men have a lot of intimate contact). For Leye, this translated into her being in her private world, always looking downwards (her father, Sender, describes her as walking 'with her eyes down-cast' (*The Dybbuk*, 1992: 12). As rehearsals progressed, I introduced repeated sequences of simple actions, starting from walking, sitting, and standing. This allowed individuals to explore how they moved in a range of modes and spaces. The first week ended with circle dancing, practising a sliding mode of striding across the floor, and collective work on creating the synagogue space with shokeling, the rhythmic forward and back swaying of prayer, within which we then improvised.

The 'close community' spirit, which Taylor described (1992), was supported by this group work with the company, especially in the first exploratory rehearsals. Along with the notion of musicality, one of the hallmarks of Gardzienice's approach is the concept of mutuality, which for them is about working in close relation to others, either on a microscale in a specific mutuality training exercise conducted in pairs, or on the macroscale of how the company coexist with the locals in the village of Gardzienice itself or on their rural travels (Allain, 1997: 59–78 and 21–30). Staniewski has rather playfully defined mutuality as the 'closeness effect', contrasting this with Bertolt Brecht's concept of estrangement/*Verfremdungseffekt*, though that has a very different focus and purpose from the kinds of practices about which Staniewski is speaking.

We never worked in general terms on 'being Jewish', whatever that might mean, only ever exploring very specific aspects of religious or cultural practices. We regularly shokeled until it became second nature. We made sure that the cast was familiar and comfortable with their costumes, which are complex and detailed, including prayer shawls, skullcaps or kippahs, and sidelocks.

We sang Jewish songs together and danced. For Hasidic Jews, music and dance can be forms of prayer, and although I do not recall now if any of our cast were practising Jews (actor and musical director Livingstone was from Jewish heritage but not practising), we enacted the forms irrespective of anyone's religious or spiritual beliefs, trying only to understand and portray what is described in the play text. Given the limited lived Jewish experience amongst the cast, we sought more objective cultural and religious expertise in several ways, including our fieldwork in Ukraine: through the dance session with Maman; by commissioning a revised translation by dramaturg Mira Rafalowicz; by consulting with David Schneider, actor, comedian and Yiddish theatre and language expert; and through discussions with London-based Rabbi Rabinowicz, including during rehearsals. Rabinowicz kindly loaned us Jewish religious materials for scenic décor and props for the performance. We thereby tried to ground our research and practice in expertise, Jewish and theatre-based, wherever possible.

I led movement work to support individuals other than Pearce. With John Shrapnel, who played Reb Azriel, we worked physically on his age, his slow speed, and his heaviness. We tried to physically understand and embody more subtle aspects like his meditative qualities, how he might sense things with his back with 360-degree awareness, and how he might even 'see' things with his eyes shut. By focusing on physical aspects like Azriel's tempo and how he senses and sees, we opened practical possibilities that might invoke his wisdom, his ability to read situations, and his capacity as a rabbinical leader. We asked how the qualities of such a senior religious figure like him might manifest, but tried to avoid cultural or other stereotyping. Building from the solo work, we then explored how others interact, for example, by playing with the physical distance that they give him by not entering his personal space.

In rehearsals, such behaviours can be explored individually by the actors as they start to interpret the role, beginning from the character's description in the play text. This work can also be done under the watchful guidance of movement specialists. We attempted to reconstruct 'a Hasidic Jewish enclave in turn-of-the-century Eastern Europe', as Taylor described it (*Independent*, 1992). Most reviews confirmed that we were successful in this aim, even though some found the play hard going and the content too obscure, in the first Act especially. Carole Woddis wrote that 'The music and dance sequences by Ben Livingstone and Paul Allain have a marvellous lyric naturalism about them – a quality that is striking too in the acting' (*What's On*, 1992). Michael Billington stated that 'The whole cast of 24 bring to life this Chagall-like community steeped in memory, tradition and a belief that we can be happy in the universe even if we are miserable in the world. But I was deeply impressed by the ensemble dedication and directorial detail' (*Guardian*, 1992). I believe that my movement directing played a crucial part in this achievement.

Live Like Pigs (1958)

John Arden's play shares something in common with *The Dybbuk* in charting in detail a community in crisis and on the edge of change. However, its tragi-comic style draws from popular culture and Bertolt Brecht, with larger-than-life characters and almost absurd situations. One of the more Brechtian aspects is Arden's use of song, as academic John Russell Taylor noted: 'Song plays an important part in Arden's work, and is almost always used quite non-realistically' (Russell Taylor, 1963: 77).

The play depicts the Sawneys, a group of 'sturdy beggars' as Arden calls them, who are forcibly moved from their caravan into a housing estate in the North of England. They then clash with the local family, the Jacksons, who are initially friendly to the newcomers. It ends with the Sawneys being chased by a mob out of the house and away from the area. In the Introductory Note to the 1967 published edition, Arden states that he 'intended it to be not so much a social document as a study of differing ways of life brought sharply into conflict' (Russell Taylor, 1963: 101). When first performed in 1958 at the Royal Court Theatre, it divided its audience and critics, who found its ambiguity troubling as it does not value one community over the other. Who lives like 'pigs'? Arden leaves this question open.

As with *The Dybbuk*, Gardzienice-based ensemble practice helped to create the vivid physical and vocal energy needed to depict this nomadic community, which includes characters such as Big Rachel, played by Kathryn Hunter, or Col, her son, played by a then-unknown Jude Law. The play also contains a possession, though of a completely different order. Rachel is 'Possessed by her rage, and her words are interspersed with sheer animal noises'. She is even 'foaming at the mouth' (Arden, 2014: 178). My main task as movement director, collaborating with Mitchell, was twofold: to assist with the portrayal of the Traveller characters' volatility and emotionality through their physical interactions; and to help the cast enact vibrant celebrations and harsh violence, for example, when Sailor and Rachel fight (Arden, 2014: 122). We wanted this to impact the audience viscerally in the small upstairs studio theatre at the Royal Court.

A key performance moment is Col's dance (Arden, 2014: 115, 118), described by Arden with some important details: 'very strange barbarous fashion, flinging out his arms and legs and whooping' (Arden, 2014: 118). The dance developed out of movement exercises and one-to-one work with Law, but was also informed by research into Kent's Roma. Mitchell and I consulted with Simon Evans, an expert and author on British Roma and Travellers (Evans, 2004). This gave us insights into how Travellers dance, sometimes using a sheet of tin which they throw onto the floor to create an instantaneous, resonant miniature stage. Another useful source was *Into the West* (1992), an Irish film which features Gabriel Byrne's 'gypsy' dance by a bonfire.

The Sawneys were a necessary focus because of their distinctiveness, but all cast members had to find the animal in their character: from Sailor as a limping 'poor old horse', as he is described, to Rosie the 'dirty bitch', as Rachel calls her (Arden, 2014: 111), skulking like a dog in a box. Arden's *dramatis personae* gives two or three lines of mostly physical description for every character and some indicators about their temperaments.

As well as finding their animals, we worked on widening the actors' movement vocabulary: we sought strong, big, expansive, very fast, rhythmical, and musical movement. We played with being either light or heavy on the feet and staying low to the ground and agile. Temperamentally, the Sawneys shift quickly from loving to fighting, although overall, they are a close-knit community. I helped the Sawneys become dance-lovers, doing rhythmical exercises for the feet and clapping. James Christopher described the production as 'sinewy' with an 'impressive cast' (*Time Out*, 1993).

We explored proxemics in the second rehearsal to understand how the Travellers often touched each other and the effects on them of small, cramped interior spaces, potentially creating claustrophobia. Previously, they had spent as much time as possible outdoors. The characters work hard, manually, with Sailor's jobs being, according to Rosie, to 'wind a crane, dig drains, heaving barrels [...] then into the boozer till closing – likely fight a pair o' men into canal dock' (Arden, 2014: 111). How does such a life affect the body? The characteristics shared by the Travellers were then set in contrast to the spatial dynamics and behaviours of the doctor, the official, and the Jacksons, their new neighbours. One source that helped us understand the northern lifestyle and the poverty was Alan Clarke's film *Rita Sue and Bob Too* (1987), set on a very poor estate in Bradford in the north of England.

As mentioned, Arden's scenes are interspersed in a Brechtian manner with ballads, one of which opens the play. Whereas in *The Dybbuk*, song was mostly for prayer and was intrinsic to the action, here it became both a framing and linking device between scenes, something that was repeated in *Henry VI: The Battle for the Throne* (RSC, 1994), explored in Section 3. In his introduction, Arden discusses the need to integrate the ballads and the single balladeer (as he conceived it) into the overall text: if this cannot be done, the role should be cut, he suggests. We ensured integration by singing the songs collectively, following Gardzienice's practice of choral song work. The ballad that opened the play was set to the tune of the traditional Newcastle mining song *Byker Hill*, onto which we layered the opening lines, spoken loudly together by the cast whenever they stopped at the front of the stage to face the audience.

In rehearsal, we combined singing with big stamps, jumps, and crossing movements with some elements of Hungarian folk dance: landing on the inside of the feet, clicking the fingers, clapping hands, having loose fingers, and watching your feet move when facing each other. Gardzienice's lively and vigorous ensemble practice, combined with other elements such as chi kung, suited the material. It assisted our attempt to go beyond stereotypes and create onstage a vivid Traveller culture, something which is all too rarely depicted in the British theatre, especially by non-Irish playwrights like Arden.

The performance was well received at the time but had little lasting impact. Michael Coveney praised 'The action, beautifully poised between farce and tragedy, [...] punctuated by vigorous bursts of *a capella* folk song' (*Observer*, 1993). It gets even less attention than *The Dybbuk* in Fowler's 2021 book, with just a passing mention. There is no video record or publicly available documentation other than a brief note on the Royal Court Theatre's Living Archive pages, although the photos for two productions of the play presented there are mistakenly switched, and the information is incomplete (Royal Court Living Archive). One very brief review exists open access online (Royal Court at 60, 2016), although fourteen positive reviews (with a critical exception) are gathered in the subscription-only *Theatre Record* (October–November 1993: 1225–1228). Perhaps this passing interest can be attributed in part to the fact that the play is rarely performed, its agitprop style probably unappealing to contemporary directors. This is regrettable, with Travellers and Roma still marginalised and discriminated against across the UK, and homelessness still an urgent, large-scale problem. Surely the 'astonishing relevance of its themes', that Louise Doughty identified in 1993, has not dissipated (*Mail on Sunday*, 1993)?

Conclusion

In both examples, techniques and processes inspired and informed by the Polish theatre company Gardzienice were used to stage these two plays in London in well-known venues with high-calibre casts and production teams. Concepts such as mutuality and musicality, and Gardzienice's energetic approach to bodywork and song were introduced in the form of intensive exercises and training during rehearsals through my role as movement director. This helped the depiction of these two unusual communities.

In such anthropologically determined creative processes, ethical issues and questions about authority and representation inevitably arise. As Fowler noted, these issues would be even more rigorously interrogated today, when questions about consent, colour-blind or colour-conscious casting, and the ethics of playing certain roles abound, informed by lively debates and guidelines drawn up by professional bodies. In 2021, Equity was establishing a network of actors from Gypsy, Roma, or Traveller backgrounds to help address their underrepresentation in the industry (BBC, 2021). Solutions to complex problems in some areas are only just beginning to surface. In others, positions and principles are more established.

I do not wish to explore these arguments further here, just as I do not wish to enter into consideration of the accusations of abuse that have more recently circulated around Gardzienice and Jerzy Grotowski. My work with Gardzienice and both productions examined predates these discussions by decades and were created in another time and theatre culture. This is not to excuse any unethical practices or misrepresentations but is more complex than I have space for here. For both plays, we assiduously attempted to portray the cultures with respect and compassion, supported by detailed research in the field and on the page and through close collaboration with experts. We then used rigorous movement processes to inhabit and portray individual and collective lives on stage.

A common concern today is that, economics or practicalities aside, nervousness about the 'rights' of representation might deter artists from staging such important works. Self-censorship can be a major inhibitor. It is heartening, then, to discover the pleasingly open approaches outlined by a leading British Jewish casting agency (Wagner, 2023, and Wagner, nd) and Jewish Olivier-nominated actor Simon Lipkin. I leave the last words to Lipkin, spoken on his nomination for Best Actor for playing Fagin in *Oliver!* (2024) in London: 'I don't always believe that you have to play the thing that you are – I wouldn't care if someone not Jewish was playing Fagin. I'd just want them to play it with respect and knowledge' (Lipkin in *The Stage*, 2025). I hope it is clear how movement can help with this task.

2 Making Worlds on Stage

In the previous section, I analysed how movement could function in rehearsals to help a cast embody other cultures, focusing on *The Dybbuk* and *Live Like Pigs*, depicting Jewish and Traveller communities respectively. With *The Dybbuk*, attention was paid to other ways of interpreting the play text across theatre and film to contextualise our realist interpretation. I also explained how our production was supported by fieldwork in Ukraine, collaboration with Jewish cultural experts, and detailed literary and historical research. *Live Like Pigs* involved similar rehearsal processes and some consultation, though not fieldwork, to create the vivid Traveller characters. In both texts, specific aspects were scripted or at least mentioned, such as the possession, the exorcism, rituals, dances, or fights; much else, including characterisation, was largely open to interpretation.

In this section, I will look initially at plays where there are seemingly no overt or large-scale movement demands, at least in the given texts, and how movement may then have other functions, including group formation. Struan Leslie has described how, from his perspective, the work of the movement director 'should be invisible' (in Cornford and Svich, 2020: 243). His premise is that the mise en scène should have holistic integrity, where no single element stands out. However, as the previous section demonstrated, movement is often very evident in performance, even if its function, role, or the process by which it has been arrived at is little understood. As Leslie himself has clarified, dance sequences usually signal the input of a movement director or other specialist. But even aspects beyond choreography or dance are often mentioned in reviews by critics and are presumably observed by audiences, too. As I have discussed, this has often arisen from practices explored and physical choices made in rehearsal. Is movement so invisible?

This question of what is visible or invisible also pertains to the thorny and much-discussed question of what is and what makes an ensemble. A frequent observation of Mitchell's early work was that it had a noticeable ensemble spirit. Nicola Robertson mentioned the 'controlled ensemble work' in *Arden* (*Time Out*, 1990), Mitchell and my first production together, for which I was listed as Physical Trainer/Assistant Director. In a review of Maxim Gorky's *Vassa Zheleznova*, for which I briefly worked on movement, Michael Billington stated that 'the acting, in fact, has unusual ensemble strength' (*Guardian*, 1990). Alastair Macaulay noted of *Ghosts* that 'the actors play as a true ensemble' (*Financial Times*, 1993). What constitutes an ensemble might not be explicitly visible, but it can often be felt, both within the group and even by an audience – in a sense of togetherness and collaboration, shared focus and intent, active listening and responsiveness, and rhythmical cohesion. These are just some hallmarks of strong ensemble work and explain the name of one of the UK's most successful theatre companies, Complicité, which has often been celebrated for its tight ensemble practice.

John Britton's and Duška Radosavljević's edited collections on ensemble (both 2013) explore such factors. Understandably, though, they struggle to settle on a clear definition beyond the self-evident notion that an ensemble can be defined by institutional parameters or structures, such as the fact that the actors have worked together for a sustained period. This was not the case in any of our productions, although Mitchell did gradually start to work repeatedly with several actors like Kristin Hutchinson (*Live Like Pigs*) and Angus Wright (*The Dybbuk*), in part to benefit and build from mutual understanding and familiarity. Our work with the RSC might, on the face of it, be considered an exception, as the company then prided itself on being an ensemble with long-term contracts for a stable group of actors.[2] Many have, however, questioned what this meant in practice and how manifest the ensemble spirit was. In addition, for *The Dybbuk* and *Henry VI*, we largely cast new actors rather than those from the already existing pool, as was required for *Ghosts*.

It has always been a vital aspect of my contribution to rehearsals to try to unite the cast through physical work, movement, and exercises. This is encouraged through expecting fast responses to impulses or instructions, extensive group and choral work, breathing and singing together, which encourages synchronicity, and basic acrobatics with clear technical parameters: if an actor jumps onto another's thigh, safety and the need for a stable balance dictate how it can be achieved. This builds self-confidence and trust and understanding of others as well as self-insight.

With such principles established as a foundation, I can then, working with the other team members across scenic, technical, vocal, musical and stage management areas, help to create 'the world of the play', as Mitchell calls it in her book (Chapter 10, 2009). What does she mean by this? Mitchell never defines it but emphasises that the imaginative work must have coherence, with the actors (and by extension the audience) needing collectively to believe in a 'construction', which must be shared by the whole team. My role is fundamental for ensemble-building but also helps to manifest the world of the play, with an emphasis on how the cast moves in and through the onstage space; how they use, sense, feel and exist in it; how and where they interact. This has temporal and spatial dimensions, as movement encompasses both.

Importantly, movement work helps ensure that the actors are ready for rehearsals (hence the need for daily warm-ups) and performance. Warming up is not something this Element explicitly focuses on, but it should not be disregarded that physical work can make actors fitter and more prepared for the tough demands of nightly performances, perhaps keeping them healthier too. Mitchell's performances are often long and require intense effort and concentration. The cast needs stamina. *Henry VI* had a substantial tour, with fourteen UK and fifteen overseas venues at which there were often multiple performances. The stage manager's nightly reports, accessible in the RSC Archive, reveal how frequently illness affected the production, especially as the tour progressed.

Movement in rehearsals supported and developed different approaches to acting across a range of forms. Case studies discussed in this section include

---

[2] Michael Boyd, Artistic Director of the RSC from 2002–2012, the decade after Mitchell and my work there, has discussed ensemble and the company, stating how it was inspired by 'the great East European ensembles of the late '50s/early '60s'. A key criterion for him was the longevity of time spent together (Boyd, 2010).

Henrik Ibsen's *Ghosts* (RSC, 1993), Githa Sowerby's *Rutherford and Son* (National Theatre, 1994), and Ernst Toller's expressionist *The Machine Wreckers* (National Theatre, 1995), for all of which I was movement director for Mitchell. The diversity of these plays' genres and periods might suggest that very different approaches would be needed for each. To examine if this was indeed the case, I will build on Section 1 to consider in more detail how movement relates to stage space as well as other aspects of acting.

Ghosts (1881)

In *Live Like Pigs*, the Travellers had an atypical relationship with domestic spaces. Ibsen's *Ghosts* requires a very different understanding of and approach to stage space, informed as it is by the harsh Scandinavian weather with long periods of winter darkness in an age before central heating – if one attempts a period reenactment as we did. Whereas *Live Like Pigs* depicted nomads struggling to adapt to an indoor environment, here, the enclosed, dark interior domestic space heightens Ibsen's exploration of how a family can become imprisoned by its past sins, transgressions, and moral codes. In both texts, the characters experience feeling entrapped, but they react in very different ways.

Ghosts has a very rich subtext and undercurrents, full of undisclosed secrets and feelings. With its small cast of five, it revolves around Mrs Alving and her son Oswald, who has inherited syphilis, of which he is initially unaware until a medical consultation. It has most likely been passed on from his dissolute father. Mrs Alving's maid, Regina, is the lustful father's daughter, conceived through his sexual liaison with a servant. This is revealed during the play to both Regina and Oswald, who had himself started showing interest in her, his half-sister, and was planning to run away to Paris with her. The house is full of ghosts, as Mrs Alving says at the very end of Act One. She suddenly realises, through the kerfuffle that she and Pastor Manders hear in the room next door, that Oswald is replicating her late husband's libidinous behaviour by approaching and presumably grabbing or groping Regina.

Our task was not about directing where, how, and when the actors should move, other than in the most general terms, guided by what is stipulated in the stage directions or determined by the script. After all, as Fowler helpfully reminds us, 'Mitchell doesn't do 'blocking', insisting that the shape of a room determines where things happen' (Fowler, 2021: 29). Blocking can fix, impose, and restrict, meaning actors are less able or inclined to make spontaneous or intuitive choices. This is why I avoid describing my practice as choreography. Our process was rather about helping the actors understand how the social, cultural, political, and natural environment impacts the body, and forms and shapes interactions with those closest to us, as well as strangers. This is what naturalism explores *par excellence*, epitomised in a play like *Ghosts*. This needs to be grounded through both theoretical and embodied research for the actors to gather enough intelligence about the period and its conventions and practices to make informed choices, with a sense of 'lived experience'. The team needs to create a total, homogenous space, Mitchell's 'world', which all actors occupy equally, rather than one defined by individual preferences or whims.

Parameters are initially fixed by the set designer, who, in the case of *Ghosts*, was Mitchell's frequent collaborator Vicki Mortimer. The small studio space of The Other Place suited this play. The actors must then make the fictional space familiar, as though it is their actual home or environment. Movement and acting involve two things: visible trajectories, actions, and patterns, but also what the actor does not do or where they do not go. We worked on both stillness and restraint, movement and impulses, sometimes withheld. The inner and outer worlds need to connect.

My input as movement director was limited. A longer engagement was initially planned, but in the end, I was only available for the first week. We practised slow movement and calming breath work, using a chi kung sequence to which I have returned repeatedly and that has no direct relation to Gardzienice's work, to help create the quiet, sustained tension of the highly charged domestic situation. We explored resistance and withholding inner movement and feelings so that they did not manifest externally. After our initial explorations, I handed over responsibility to lead practical sessions and warm-ups to the youngest member of the cast, Alexandra Gilbreath, who played Regina. This maintained a focus on the body and space in rehearsals.

Michael Billington noted of the performance that 'the main revelation was the influence of climate on character: Mitchell and her designer, Vicki Mortimer, had both travelled widely in Norway and caught perfectly that country's amazingly swift transitions from golden sunlight to sodden, inspissated gloom' (*Guardian*, 2023). The light is especially important, since the play ends with Oswald looking into and welcoming the rarely seen morning sun. This comes immediately after he gets agreement from his mother that she will administer a morphine overdose when he has seriously degenerated from syphilis. In his review at the time, Billington wrote that 'The strength of Mitchell's production is that it not only exploits the space's intimacy but also explores the characters' complexity' (*Guardian*, 1993). Space and acting are inexorably linked.

The movement work helped the actors focus on character details as well as supported them in building a sense of Norway's 'gloomy fjord landscape' (*Ghosts*, 27), the downpour (Act One), the mist (Act Two) and the night-time setting for the final Act Three: 'Outside it is dark, with only a faint glow from the fire in the background' (83). An atmosphere and a 'world' are created by people and how they behave, as much as by sound, lighting, and set. One must move cautiously in the dark, even in a familiar space. Human sounds echo in wood-lined rooms, with movement and noise easily perceptible, as discovered by Mrs Alving and Pastor Manders at the end of Act One.

Many critics commented on the claustrophobia created by this dark room, which was often surrounded by sheets of incessant rain, realised through sound, the set with its gutter and drains, and the acting. John Peter commented that 'The room is like a compression chamber. I have never heard such silences' (*Sunday Times*, 1993). Margaret Ingram echoed this: 'its claustrophobia is almost palpable' with 'an intensity of concentration which never falters' (*Stratford Herald*, 1993). Together, we created a production of 'explosive power' (*Daily Telegraph*, 1993), as Charles Spencer described it.

Rutherford and Son (1912)

Rutherford and Son has similar family preoccupations and themes to *Ghosts*. They also share common aspects in their potential staging, with claustrophobic, single-room, domestic, interior settings. Both *Rutherford*, as we called it for short, and *Machine Wreckers* (National Theatre, 1995) are concerned with work and how those with power control and subordinate others to their money-making desires. We had to show how various types of labour, glassmaking and weaving respectively, affect the body and highlight class differences and how they become manifest in various behaviours and physicalities.

As well as these priorities, for *Rutherford* rehearsals, for which I was present mainly in the first two weeks, I aimed to assist the actors to embody the characters, give focus to spatial considerations, and help them interpret textual indicators such as the many involuntary movements mentioned in the stage directions. My short article on 'Movement Directing', written at the time, describes my contribution and gives a good account of the process we followed (Allain, 1994). It also usefully describes chi kung, with its emphasis on form, breath, centring, calmness, stillness, and quiet energy, a useful counterpoint to the extrovert Polish approach.

The play is about a family in Gateshead, Northumbria, ruled over by patriarch and glass factory owner John Rutherford, who controls his family as tightly as he commands his workforce. The action all occurs in the living room of their large Edwardian house, an everyday domestic site. Following similar naturalist dramas of the period, the piece comprises many small actions and habits which intersperse the characters' heated interactions, including pipe-smoking, the pulling down of blinds, and the laying of the table. Much of this daily activity is suggested in the long stage directions, which also indicate emotional responses and occasionally even specific movements. Many of these chores are done by Rutherford's daughter Janet as she slavishly maintains order or serves her father's needs under the watchful eye of his sister Ann.

Janet is in love with Rutherford's lead worker, Martin, who, when challenged about this by Rutherford, stays loyal to his 'master' rather than abandoning him and his work for Janet. Disappointed and with no way back after Rutherford confronts her about the affair, Janet leaves the house towards the end of the play. Her brothers, John and Dick, a vicar, have similarly difficult relations with their father. At one point, Rutherford asks the latter why he was even born, and he manipulates Martin to hand over John's possibly successful recipe for a more efficient glass-making process. This is the only card John has over his father, which he had hoped would release him and his wife Mary, from his father's stranglehold. With no options left, John steals money from Rutherford and runs away, probably heading overseas. The play ends with Mary bargaining with Rutherford Senior for her and John's son Tony to later take over the firm in exchange for Rutherford looking after his every need and education for ten years. The arch-capitalist Rutherford, cornered and with few possibilities to ensure that his life's work will continue, has been outsmarted and outmanoeuvred by a woman and Southerner from a lowly background – an office worker in London. Reluctantly, he agrees to her proposition.

In my article, I wrote that 'It is impossible to quantify how my work affected the performance' (Allain, 1994). Critical responses suggest otherwise. Just as the precise spatial work which we had conducted for *Ghosts* was noted by Billington, several reviews of *Rutherford* commented on this aspect. Billington again was impressed by the 'Claustrophobic intensity' (*Guardian*, 1994). Paul Taylor noted the 'Vast alienating gaps between the pieces of furniture' (*Independent*, 1994). John Peter observed how

> The director, Katie Mitchell, has him (Rutherford) march in straight to his desk down stage, looking at nobody, his mind entirely concentrated on the papers which await his attention. It is not that Rutherford has decided to ignore people in the room; rather, for him, they are pieces of furniture which you expect to find much as you left them. (*Sunday Times*, 1994: 20)

When we first meet Rutherford, the stage directions indicate that 'There is a distinct change in the manner of the whole family as he comes in and walks straight to his desk as if the door has scarcely interrupted his walk' (*Rutherford and Son*, 23; all play citations are from my personal rehearsal copy of the text). The sequence follows Sowerby's textual directions but was enacted with such conviction that it stood out for Peter. The reviews attest to the work we did in rehearsal to create a specific domestic environment with its oppressive claustrophobia.

Taylor's comment is especially interesting considering some of the exercises we conducted. Each actor had to determine and then become familiar with their character's rhythm so that they were able to move in the space as though blind. Mary moves quickly. Rutherford has precision in movement and is definite, walking straight, as Peter observed. Ann fusses about. Martin is simple in manner and bearing. Janet is listless, lacking desire, her movement described in the opening stage directions as 'slipshod and aimless' (1). At one point in the text, listening intently, Janet raises her eyes 'almost for the first time' (19). She steals looks, glances.

We took this investigation further, with one cast member shutting their eyes to be led slowly by another: they had to recognise each other's rhythms and where each person was in the space through sound and proprioception alone. We established the concept that each object or piece of furniture has an aura around it linked to the person who uses or occupies it the most. Rutherford's desk was an item, as was Ann's chair by the fire. We asked ourselves: are the objects magnets and the people metal, which we then tried to enact? We asked where the heat and light sources were. To help create a sense of a physically cold space, reflecting the emotional dynamics, we located the fireplace as a single source of heat. We questioned where the characters might feel comfortable in the space. Who sits where? How high is the ceiling? How do you behave on your own, starting with one person and then adding in others in different sequences to see how a character's comfortable solitude dissipates?

Within this world, we played with silence and stillness, both of which could become entrenched out of fear of upsetting the status quo or of violence – a kind of animal fear. We described as animal paths the characters' movements around the room, making them highly sensitised to where to avoid. Early in the script, there is at one point the simple stage direction '(Movement)' (10), a gift for us. We played Grandmother's Footsteps, fostering attention to others, how to hold back, have control, and then release, encouraging heightened awareness of where your own and others' bodies are at any moment. This game worked best when Rutherford was 'grandmother'. The stillness in the room could sometimes be too much for the characters to bear, leading to unease and fidgeting. We explored this quality and how far it could be stretched before it is broken. Chi kung helped with this, especially its final calming breathing sequence, which ends in a centred, relaxed stillness from which movement can then arise.

Irving Wardle wrote that the 'Production excels whenever the action subsides into tight-lipped festering silences and the stunted characters speak only to put one another down' (*Independent on Sunday*, 1994). Nicholas de Jongh picked up on this mood of 'unrelenting gloom', noting that it was an 'Atmospherically vivid and impassioned production' (*Evening Standard*, 1994: 7). Across its run time of 2 hours and 44 minutes – initially with two intervals that were subsequently changed to just one – the interior domestic silence was very occasionally punctured by recorded sound effects of distant thunder or rooks. These briefly took the audience to the world outside the Rutherford house, a world into which the three children all eventually escape.

Linked to this silence and stillness was the idea of impulse and restraint. We conducted an improvisation where the space is completely still and silent except for just one person moving – to see how everyone else might react. The actors had to walk and then run on impulse. At what point is the decision made to run? Why, and why then? At one point, John is 'uneasy and consequently rather swaggering' (27), revealing a bravado which is just a front. What happens when Rutherford bangs his fist on the table? This opened up the involuntary movements often described in the stage directions, which I discuss in my article. The fist-banging leads to 'dead silence on this, broken only by an involuntary nervous movement from the rest of the family' (32).

Touch is barely mentioned in the script, either in stage directions or by inference in the text. In Act Three, Janet 'clings' (76) to Martin and later, just before he leaves for good, John 'takes [Mary] in his arms' and she 'clings' to him (87). The actors carried each other around, feeling the burden of the weight of another. They worked on resistance and what that feels like. In another exercise sequence, the actors walked towards someone, letting their emotions grow as they advanced, then touched them. This was the only time we explicitly worked with emotions concerning movement, though we never dictated or even suggested what these might be. This was for the actors to discover for themselves.

There were also specific character traits or past experiences to be embodied. Mary and John both had ill health due to poor working conditions and an accident (John). The environment and their histories were etched on their bodies. To understand their daily labour, the actors had to find a work action, repeat it, analyse it, discover where the weight and any stress sat, consider whether it flowed, and ascertain which muscles carried the load. This echoes Rudolf von Laban's work on Effort Actions, though we never overtly used or referenced his practices.

The world of a play is enshrined in a text, but that text is just a template that needs to be brought to life. Mitchell's inclusion of a movement director in her team for *Rutherford* might, on the face of it, seem unnecessary or a luxury, given that the play is a familiar Edwardian domestic drawing room drama. Yet Sowerby has written a detailed, precise, well-crafted, and minutely shaped play of interactions, much of which includes silences, stillness, involuntary micro-gestures, as well as everyday habits and chores. The Gateshead house is not a world of possessions, dancing, song, or fighting, as is *The Dybbuk* or *Live Like Pigs*. Rather, it is the opposite, one where actions, movements, impulses, and emotions are mostly withheld, as in *Ghosts*. The characters' painful familial tensions and conflicts surface from moment to moment and are enshrined in their physicalities. This requires subtle acting, for which the cast needed to make their discoveries first, for themselves, before trying to make them legible to the audience. My role assisted with this process. It is gratifying that the production was nominated for three Olivier Awards, including two for acting: Bob Peck (Rutherford) as Best Actor and Bríd Brennan (Janet) as Best Actress in a Supporting Role.

In the National Theatre's Platform that was set up for this production, Genista McIntosh noted how 'Some people might be surprised to see a movement director credited for a production of *Ghosts* or a production of *Rutherford and Son*, but there is one' (Platform, 1994). Mitchell, referencing my presence in the room and my role, described our 'very, very gentle, not very often, very, very specific work, just to do with breathing, which was only in the early stages of rehearsals, but nonetheless, for me, crucial' (Platform, 1994). Responding from the auditorium to Mitchell's direct question asking whether this was helpful for the actors, June Watson, who played Ann, corroborated that it was very useful. McIntosh summarises by saying that

> It's just interesting to know that you can use those techniques that you have evolved through a number of other plays, just as effectively. Dealing with something, which from our point of view, seems different, a play in a room, as it were, where people aren't doing movement here in the same way that they are if they were Women of Troy. (Platform, 1994)[3]

McIntosh's point is that some plays seem to require a movement-based approach, while others do not. I would counter by saying that all plays deploy bodies in space and time and therefore require specialist movement input, even if the need is not explicit in the text. A good example might be Samuel Beckett's *Happy Days* (1961), where Winnie is trapped in a mound of earth with movement limited to the top half of her body only. Her 'dance' and movements might

---

[3] McIntosh mentions *Women of Troy* as Mitchell had directed it at The Gate, London, in July 1991, for which Emma Rice led the chorus and movement work. Rice's work was significantly inspired by Gardzienice, with whom she had spent months as an actor.

happen on a microscale, but they need to be worked on and considered as seriously and thoroughly as choral work for a Greek tragedy. Movement is not just about dancing and fighting, both of which usually belong to the domain of specialist choreographers, dance experts, or fight directors.

In the closing Question and Answer section of the Platform, an audience member observed that 'The actors in *Rutherford* have this incredible ability to create stillness between actions, sort of like a counterpoint' (Platform, 1994). He then asked: 'Was that specific to this play? I suspected it might have been something about the way you worked with them' (Platform, 1994). Mitchell responds by putting it down firstly to the playwright, Sowerby, writing lots of silences, as well as the actors and their bravery in trusting such moments.

I would suggest that this confidence and those choices also arose from the movement exercises and practices that I introduced to the cast. The stillness clearly cannot be solely attributed to me, as Mitchell suggests, but it is a contributory factor, though one that is easily forgotten or overlooked, as Mitchell's focus on just the two other aspects testifies. Movement might possibly be invisible, never more so than in stillness on stage, but that does not mean it is not important. In his review of *Arden*, Alasdair Macaulay observed that 'stillness and movement are memorable: there are excellent effects, both of minuscule detail of gesture and of startling violence' (*Financial Times*, 1990). Stillness can only exist in relation to movement and must come from somewhere. In addition, stillness is movement. The body is only fully at rest when we die, something that makes dying or killing on stage so difficult, to be explored in the next section.

The Machine Wreckers (1922)

My work on this production, Mitchell and my last collaboration, repeated many of the processes previously discussed in this and the first section. Again, precise character observation and embodiment were required: John Webley with his hunched back, an adult playing a very young girl, and beggars and starving children are just three examples. A significant difference from earlier collaborations, however, was that the play is expressionist. Many characters in the large *dramatis personae* are figurative and representational rather than psychologically rounded characters, and they often have few lines, if any. This would suggest that a different process might be required for such a radical departure from naturalism, the dominant mode for Mitchell's previous work. This was not the case, though, as will be explained.

The Machine Wreckers is set in Nottingham in the early nineteenth century and depicts a group of workers who fear being replaced in their weaving by seemingly inevitable mechanisation. Much of the play shows the strikers' protests and debates about whether to destroy the machine, featuring the key figure of Ned Ludd, after whom the Luddites or machine wreckers were named. It also shows the privileged position of the factory owners and those defending them, including the military. In the end, the workers revolt against this process and attack the machine.

The text includes fights, the celebratory lifting of Jimmy onto a striking worker's shoulders, group protests, and the mobbing in the final scene that leads to Jimmy being beaten to death. Cultural aspects we needed to understand and embody included the effects of extended manual work on the body and the impact of poverty and starvation. In a newspaper article that she wrote about a fieldwork trip with the cast to Nottingham, Mitchell references a meeting with Mandy Wilson, who once worked at the Stocking Weavers Museum in Ruddington:

> [Wilson] tells us that most of the stocking-weavers would have suffered from stoops, shortsightedness, chest complaints, and calloused thumbs from the work [...] We have talked a great deal in the rehearsal room about the working conditions of the Luddites in the 19th century, but it is the concrete reality of this visit that brings it home to the cast in a practical and sensual fashion – I can see the actors stooping backs, or flexing muscles as Mandy weaves. (*Independent*, 1995)

The fieldwork in Ukraine for *The Dybbuk* did not include actors for financial and logistical reasons, but it is important to understand the potential value of such a process, as identified here.

Academic Marvin Carlson described the piece's style in a review article: 'even while occasionally quoting expressionistic devices, [she] emphasized the everyday human situations, often in an almost naturalistic manner' (*Western European Stages*, 1995: 57). He writes that it is mainly naturalistic with 'expressionistic touches and bridges' (58). He praises both the 'intimate scenes' with their 'intensity, psychological depth, and attention to physical detail that is usually associated with naturalism' and the 'mass scenes, impressively staged by Mitchell' (*Western European Stages*, 1995: 57). He is grateful for the play's revival. I do not want to linger on definitions of naturalism and realism and their relationship to Mitchell's work, a topic explored extensively elsewhere (see Fowler, 2021: 23–40 and Solga and Rebellato in Fowler, 2018). Mitchell's interest in exploring the boundaries of naturalist theatre, sometimes even going against what might traditionally be considered the genre of the play, then led to her 'live cinema' work, as she explored how to do this with other media. Rather than defining such complex terms, I wish instead to account for my work on the play and how it responded to both stylistic aspects of the production.

Other critics praised the production. Richard Hornby believed that 'She handled groups masterfully, while moving the action forward with drive and flow' (*The Hudson Review*, 1995: 645). John Peter wrote that 'The acting style is a craggy burnished realism; the movement is balanced between realistic and the heavily sculptural'. It was a 'Superbly disciplined and sensitive production of a difficult dated play' (*Sunday Times*, 1995). Just as Taylor had praised her *Dybbuk* for its realism, Billington noted that 'She has a talent for scrupulously recreating the past. [. . .] At its best when it sticks closest to real life' (*Guardian*, 1995). Many were less impressed and found the 1922 translation by Ashley Dukes reinforced the play's didactic and old-fashioned nature, concurring with Peter's view of it being 'dated'. Some found it dull, the characters one-dimensional, and the expressionist moments lacking. Most found it overly long and awkwardly polemical.

In rehearsals, I led Gardzienice-based choral dancing and movement, much of it in collaboration with Helen Chadwick, who created the musical score. This included the strikers' 'rough music' for a scene where a mob of strikers march, led by a fiddler, and then hang up on a gallows two guys (dummies) which represent strike-breakers (scabs). The mob then dances around them, singing 'Ba Ba black sheep' which evolves into 'Blackleg, Blackleg' (*Seven Plays*, 1936: 11). Rough music is a form of carnivalesque protest using readymade instruments such as pots and pans to show anger and dislike, making as much noise as possible. It often involves the parading and violent mockery of a victim, in our case represented by the effigies with their ram's head skulls. William Hogarth's engraving *Hudibras Encounters the Skimmington* (nd) was a vital source for us, as were ideas about the 'danse macabre' or the dance of death. In one improvisation, we led the cast out of the building in a noisy procession onto the Thames embankment at the front of the National Theatre, where we were rehearsing. In another session, we did lively circle dances and played follow my leader. We tried to discover expressionism's ecstatic, emotional aspect, shaped by the basic primitive joys of human nature, manifest in dance and music.

We countered exuberance with physical examinations of inertia, collapse, being weak, and how to use each other to get up from squatting or the floor. We asked the actors in two groups to create a street scene and then a domestic one, supported by a list that we had compiled of adjectives that are used in the play. All this fed into forging a believable world. The process seems to have helped, according to at least one reviewer. Nicholas de Jongh considered that 'the scenes showing the hungry, despairing victims of mechanisation, still hit home and have messages for today' (*Evening Standard*, 1995).

A complex task was to show the community's destruction of the machine at the end of the play, reacting to the victimisation that de Jongh mentions. This was depicted by not having the loom on stage; its presence instead was created through recorded sound, lighting, and the actors' responses to it, as they looked out fearfully into the auditorium where the machine was located. Here, the production moved most forcefully towards expressionism.

Whatever the successes or failures of this choice, and the reviews were mixed, our approach again reveals that movement is about what we do not see, either what is not shown or is revealed only indirectly, as well as what is visible. The terrifying movement and noise of the machine, which increased as it was wrecked, was suggested largely by the actors' reactions, vitally supported by the sound and lighting to which they responded.

Conclusion

This section has examined three productions to show how movement can be a key element in rehearsals for a range of different styles, genres, and periods. It can offer useful spatial insights, even when movement is not explicitly written into the text. In such cases, a movement director's work can be as important as it is for plays with specific, explicit requirements. Movement is not just about fight or dance scenes but should be integral to all acting and character creation, where it can encourage bolder acting choices. It also has the added benefit of helping build an ensemble. In Section 3, we will explore examples of how movement can be used in rehearsal as a creative tool, linking this to voice and text work as well as death on stage.

3 Moving as a Creative Tool: Text, Voice, Music, and Death

The previous section examined how movement can enhance rehearsals by fostering the ensemble and generating the 'world of the play' for a range of texts. This section explores movement for two distinct aspects across three case studies: as a creative component to support textual delivery and vocal or musical work; and to assist the challenge of managing deaths and dying on stage.

The first case study is Mitchell's production of *Henry VI: The Battle for the Throne* (RSC, Stratford-upon-Avon, 1994), the only Shakespeare text she has directed (she has, though, created performances inspired by Shakespeare, such as *Ophelias Zimmer*, 2016). I will attempt to understand why this is the case and examine the piece's textual and vocal demands. As critics familiar with her work noted, this production marked a shift in her repertoire from plays presenting bleak interiors to outdoor spaces, namely battlefields across the north of

England, which we visited for the creative team's research. This spatial aspect impacts how vocal delivery might be shaped and perceived.

The second case study is Christopher Marlowe's *The Massacre at Paris* (Canterbury Cathedral Crypt, 2014), performed by second-year actors (of a two-year programme) training with Fourth Monkey Drama School, London, with me co-directing with Andrew Dawson, Creative Director of The Marlowe Theatre, Canterbury. My role here differed from other examples in this Element, yet we explicitly acknowledged and worked mainly with our respective specialisms, mine in movement and bodywork, and his in text and speech. *Massacre*, as we called it for short, was part of a small season celebrating 450 years since Marlowe's birth. Theatre performances in the Cathedral are rare, and this was an unusual collaboration between two of the city's largest institutions, in terms of footprint and significance in the city centre.

Just as *Henry VI* contains multiple deaths as part of the play's depiction of the Wars of the Roses, Marlowe's play features numerous murders. We had to understand how to kill, how to die, and what to do with the dead bodies in a non-theatre space. *Massacre* is the only performance examined in this Element that was not staged in a theatre, which impacted many decisions about movement and staging. The play has over seventeen scripted murders, most in quick succession during the St Bartholomew's Day slaughter of the Huguenots on which it is based. Death and dying on stage require careful consideration and practice, which becomes more complex in a Cathedral.

The last production investigated is a musical adaptation of Mikhail Bulgakov's *Heart of a Dog* (Major Road Theatre Company, Bradford and national tour, 1991), for which I led movement for director Al Dix. The piece's specific acting demands were to create a comic singing chorus of Soviet citizens, as well as a dog and a 'dog/man' character. A street mutt is operated on at the end of Act One to become a combined dog/human. Animal observation and incorporation are a well-recognised aspect of movement training and practice, but rarely do they lead to such complex and hybrid personifications on stage.

Henry VI: The Battle for the Throne (1591)

Benjamin Fowler has characterised the production, which depicts the struggle for power between the Houses of York and Lancaster, by noting how 'Gardzienice's influence was palpable' (Fowler, 2021: 56). He says that it crystallised questions about vocal delivery of text in her work: 'Mitchell's marriage of Shakespeare and Staniewski [Gardzienice's director] finally forced key tensions to the surface around an issue that would come to vex her reception: the enunciation of the text' (59). Battles raged both on and off stage, the latter in relation to her cast's verse-speaking.

As mentioned earlier, critics and some audience members have frequently baulked at Mitchell's vocal approach, a criticism which may sometimes be justified. Noble had responded to this concern during *The Dybbuk* previews, as noted in Section 1. In this Shakespearean case, Jonathan Firth's sotto voce approach to playing Henry VI irritated several reviewers, although some enjoyed his contemplative quietude, which they felt worked well in the small studio of The Other Place. However, the production had the biggest British and international tour ever undertaken by the RSC and was presented in diverse theatres as well as spaces like leisure centres, in a specially constructed auditorium. In addition, the criticisms cannot be considered separately from the conventions and views that circulate about Shakespeare. These would not be applied to a play by John Arden, for example. Assumptions about perceived traditions and norms of textual delivery formed the lens through which some judged the whole production.

Mitchell and I set out our initial rehearsal aims for movement for *Henry*, as we called it for short: to create choreographed battles or at least generate a sense of them happening; to assist actors with characterisation; to increase the performers' vocabulary, for example, with lifts and running; to increase their stamina; to encourage group rhythm and coordination. As with *Machine Wreckers*, in rehearsal we moved towards the idea of the audience seeing onstage only the physical and emotional consequences of major actions that had just happened or were happening off stage, in this case mostly battles.

Critic Robert Gore-Langton appreciated this decision: 'the supernatural overtones in this production are actually more pronounced than the various battles, which are conducted off-stage and to deafening sound effects – a much more satisfactory solution than the dismal Morris dancing that passes for swordfighting these days' (*Daily Telegraph*, 1994). Ironically, we had researched social dancing, including Maypole dances, inspired by paintings by Pieter Brueghel the Elder and Douglas Kennedy's *English Folk Dancing: Today and Yesterday* (1964). Yet this was mainly to familiarise ourselves with the superstitious, agrarian people of whom Shakespeare writes, with their short life spans, strong beliefs, and vivid fear of God and the devil. As one example, the actors learnt to show humility or their faith by kneeling or lying prostrate on the floor in a cross shape.

As well as trying to understand religious observances of the time, martial arts-based work was important, as we sought to make the actors familiar with war and fighting. We did rhythmic stamping and played 'Stuck-in-the-mud', creating a grounded, combat-ready stance. In one exercise, each actor had to take over and occupy another's space. The stage, covered in dirt and bark in Rae Smith's design, had to be filled by one person at a time to create a sense of battle, as actors ran, hid, or crawled across it. They sped urgently to the front and back, encouraged to use the edges of the space, which by the end of the performance were full of crosses planted in dark soil to remember the fallen. We practised Aikido's eight ways (a step and return in eight directions). We watched Akira Kurosawa's *Seven Samurai* (1954) with its mud, rain, and stillness, its slow movement followed by sudden, fast, killer blows.

We explored the heaviness of armour and weapons and how they affected the body and movement. Malcolm Ranson, often employed by the RSC, was our fight director. He offered some useful techniques and suggested fight sequences, but did not fully grasp our way of working and the intricate psychology with which Mitchell approaches directing. We had no desire to replicate stage-fighting tricks, so we adapted his input to our ends. Like Gore-Langton, Nicola Barker appreciated our choices:

> No lengthy sword fights, false blood and ludicrous battle scenes here. Mitchell's soldiers get close to kill: they hug and grapple before sliding their knives in. The play bursts open like a wound, as a clutch of young men stampede on to the stage, swords up, rusty armour rattling and clanking. This lucid production thrives on its simplicity – and minute details. (*Observer*, 1994)

Most murders happened off stage, but the performers nevertheless needed to appear accustomed to violence. Death often appeared quietly, but we also wanted to create the hectic noise of a bloody civil war.

Intrinsic to establishing a battle-ready state was the *kiai*, a word which contains *ki*, the Japanese for energy (chi in Chinese, hence chi kung – the way of energy). A *kiai* is a shout used in martial arts to focus and concentrate energy in an attack. Musical director Helen Chadwick worked on war cries and *kiais* alongside religious songs and simple chants. These helped create the 'supernatural' atmosphere to which Gore-Langton alludes. Songs in the form of chants or prayers in Latin linked scenes, as dead actors ceremonially left the stage, planting a memorial cross as they went, or as a shift indoors was indicated.

The physical work I led with the company shared much in common with that conducted for other play texts. I made no concessions for Shakespeare. Movement work with breath helped prepare the voice, supported further by Chadwick's choral singing. The textual delivery, except for the music, was Mitchell's responsibility, and no voice or text coach was brought in. The cast did, though, have access to nightly voice sessions run by the RSC's resident voice coach, but these were generic and mostly for pre-performance warming up. The inclusion of such a role might have headed off some of the more negative responses to the vocal delivery.

Mitchell has never directed another Shakespeare play. Charlotte Higgins pinpoints the likely reason: 'The play was well-received, but afterwards, she recalled, John Barton, the great Shakespearean director, took her aside and said, 'You know, it's not bad work, but every single character is miscast, the narrative is not clear and every single line of verse is mauled. Oh, and you didn't really do the battles. But other than that … ' (*Guardian*, 2016). His stinging review makes the play's great success in Stratford and on tour rather ironic, but, nevertheless, his judgment seems to have had an impact.

The Massacre at Paris (1593)

Although the two productions were twenty years apart, *Massacre* shared many aspects with *Henry*. Both are early modern dramas that depict violent battles in divided societies, fought on political or religious grounds. Today, the connection is even less surprising, as a recent edition of *Henry VI* has argued that Marlowe co-authored the play's three parts (Taylor et al., 2016).

Our main challenge with *Massacre* was to prove unfounded Sarah Munson Deat's doubt that 'in its present corrupt form it could be successfully performed today' (in Cheney, 2006: 204). Dawson and I questioned the very premise of this statement. Deat assumes that play texts have their own rules and requirements independent of performance. Can a 'corrupt' play never be staged? Does textual corruption necessarily restrict or compromise realisation on stage? Karen Quigley discusses such issues in *Performing the Unstageable* (Methuen, 2020). As well as highlighting its brevity (it is not even half the length of Marlowe's 1592 *Edward II*), scholars have criticised the play for a range of reasons: its propagandistic nature, occasional lack of clarity, and awkward mix of beautiful Marlovian poetry and doggerel. For us, this did not undermine the value of taking the challenge on, especially as Marlowe's oeuvre is limited to just seven plays in total. Two of these, *The Jew of Malta* and *Dr Faustus*, were being presented in the season alongside our production, giving us even more motivation to tackle *Massacre*.

The Massacre at Paris documents the St Bartholomew's Day massacre of Huguenots by Catholics in Paris in 1572 and its subsequent impact on French royal history in the following decades, with the downfall of the Catholic Duke of Guise as its main narrative arc. The Guise, as he is known, is the architect of the massacre and a central character in the play, with the most lines and some of the best verse. *Massacre* has twenty-six scenes, which range from long monologues to a few lines, with a cast of thirty-four named roles plus other unnamed ones. We made small textual changes and additions, partly to bring out the role of the Duchess of Guise more forcefully, and we elided some of the minor characters. For some roles, including larger ones such as Epernoun, we cast women as men, our hands tied by the reverse number of women to men in our company in relation to Marlowe's *dramatis personae*. Otherwise, we stayed close to the published text as it appears in J. B. Steane's *Complete Plays*.

It was not just the fact that the text is considered corrupt and unperformable that gave us freedom. The amateur cast, comprising training students, gave us the licence to explore and be creative. In addition, the play is rarely staged, meaning that any director is already doing something unusual by presenting it. There are few precedents with which to compare a new interpretation. Patrice Chéreau directed a 'surreal' performance in Paris in 1972 on the 400th anniversary of the massacre, which was remarkable for the fact that the stage was covered in a few inches of water into which victims sank. Clearly, we would not be able to flood Canterbury Cathedral's Crypt.

The Crypt had originally been given for worship to the Huguenots who had fled the massacre and settled as protestant refugees in Canterbury, some twenty miles from Dover, the main port of entry from France. Today, this history and their ongoing presence are recognised in the form of the Huguenot Chapel adjacent to the Crypt, where a service in French is held every Sunday at 3 PM. The play has particular significance for the city, even if, as far as we could ascertain, it had never previously been shown there. Marlowe himself was inspired to write it after hearing refugee Huguenots speaking French in the streets of Canterbury, his hometown.

As well as needing to resolve many practical issues, which I will address shortly, we were made aware of sensitivities early on. We visited the Cathedral and Crypt with the cast before rehearsals to introduce them to the space. I was quietly speaking to them in the Western Crypt about its history when I was severely reprimanded and told to be silent by a volunteer guide because this was a holy place for quiet reflection. My explanation to him about the project fell on deaf ears. It was an ironic but telling interaction, given what we were later to do there. Our response to this encounter can be seen in a short documentary film that was made about the project (*Bodies in the Crypt*, Carver, 2016).

For Anjou's coronation as King Henry III (Act Three, Scene Two), we asked for permission to have cooked food, to include the audience in an interval celebratory banquet. The suggestion was turned down by the Cathedral's Verger, who understandably deemed the smell inappropriate. My questioning moved on. The play has a succession of murders as the massacre begins in earnest. From Act One, Scenes Six–Nine especially, the Catholics go on a rampage led by the Guise, shouting 'Tue, tue, tue/kill, kill, kill' (Marlowe,

2003: 550). When I nervously asked him whether there were any conditions for our depiction of murders in such a holy place, the Verger laughed. This was not an issue at all, he smiled, reminding me of how many murders the Cathedral had seen, Becket's the most significant of them.

We wanted to show the play's violence without glorifying it, revealing how collective atrocities come to be perpetrated and even enjoyed: the cruel pleasure of violence that leads to power that is then itself overthrown in a never-ending cycle. We also wanted to emphasise what such acts cost in human terms, not diminishing their tragedy. Any musical or artistic performance event in the Cathedral is always preceded by a brief welcome speech and prayer from the current Dean, in this case, Robert Willis. His acknowledgement of the play's subject matter in the context of the millions of refugees worldwide still looking for a safe resting place prefaced and situated the piece perfectly and very movingly.

The Crypt dictated several pragmatic constraints, beyond the psychological pressure raised by the significance of this historic and sacred site and our desire to respect it. There were huge pillars at the centre of our performance space, affecting the sightlines and limiting the available stage area between the audience's surrounding chairs, which were set in an almost traverse arrangement. We did not have room for much except for a wooden butcher's block that doubled as a table. The floor was stone, leading to very echoey acoustics. With limited get-in and technical time, we decided that all sounds should be made live and electric lighting kept to a minimum. We therefore used candles, static and handheld, a rare and exciting possibility for theatre. We had to be careful with these, though, as we had rented period costumes. Petticoats, ruffs, and doublets and hose were bulky and had to be kept away from naked flames, further narrowing down the central stage space.

Limitations can turn into creative possibilities. The main stage area was situated beneath Anthony Gormley's 2011 statue *Transport*, a construction in the shape of a body made from old nails collected during repairs to the Cathedral roof. It is suspended horizontally from the ceiling and swings slowly around, wafted by indoor air currents. It both enacts and represents human movement. *Transport* is a homage to the journeys we make, physical and spiritual, particularly referencing pilgrimages: it lies above Thomas Becket's first tomb, a significant pilgrimage site for centuries. *Transport* became a reference point for our actors in performance as they looked up to it whenever mentioning God.

Beyond this main stage space, there were large 'offstage' areas behind the audience which could be used for entrances and exits as well as other activities. We could also incorporate the entire Crypt as our stage. Before the performance started, the audience was held in seats in the Western Crypt outside the Eastern

Crypt, our main auditorium. This is where Willis gave his welcome speech, which was followed by a brief symbolic enactment without text of a marriage service. This preceded the play's beginning, as the Catholic Princess Margaret of the French royal family and the Protestant King of Navarre are joined in matrimony. The audience was then led to their seats in the Eastern Crypt. Once they were settled, they were followed by those involved in the wedding who spoke the play's opening lines, which celebrate this 'union' and 'nuptial rites'. Our conception of movement encompassed how the audience entered the space and from where, not just how and where the actors moved.

One of the main tasks we faced was how to murder people and then remove their bodies, all in very close proximity to the audience (sometimes a few centimetres). There are multiple references in the stage directions to bodies being taken off and, in one case, even brought back on stage: the Lord High Admiral's corpse is carried away then reappears with two men discussing how best to dispose of it before it is hung up on a tree (stage management constructed a scaffold between an archway on which a rag doll could swing). Five or six protestants who had been praying are removed ('Exeunt with the bodies', Marlowe, 2003: 558), as is the Old Queen of Navarre, murdered by poisoned gloves.

Actors playing dead in a state of total relaxation in period costumes are heavy, a difficulty compounded by the hard floor. We piled bodies onto a low wooden cart, but even this was complicated. Otherwise, pairs carried individuals off. Rather than the 'dead' actors standing up to depart the stage as ghosts or some such stylistic representation, as we had initially anticipated and as had been our solution in *Henry VI*, we let the removal of the bodies be as true to life as possible and take the time that was needed.

We completely avoided stage blood and the complexity of stage knives, swords, and daggers, as scripted, by using blunt-ended wooden crucifixes as weapons, a provocative choice. Many protestants in the play either say or request time for one last prayer before being killed. Loreine, a Preacher, is murdered when a small bible is stuffed into his (in our case her) mouth to choke him before he is stabbed. Our decision to incorporate crucifixes was also suggested by a line when Gonzago stabs to death the already shot and wounded Admiral, saying 'Then pray unto our Lady; kiss this cross' (Marlowe, 2003: 549). Gonzago is referring to the cross that the handle and the blade of a dagger or rapier make. Even though we decided to represent this symbolically, we also wanted the murders to be felt viscerally, locating the points of impact precisely and asking the actors to respond as though stabbed. We experimented with both the moment of stabbing, of contact, and the impact on the victim, as well as how to release the body on the out-breath when dying.

One Gardzienice exercise, which proved useful for the murders, was impulse-based. Performer A stands still as B 'cuts' with a flat hand and very precise strokes specific parts of A's body. For example, A stretches their arms out straight to the sides with their hands flexed upwards at the wrist. The arm can then be cut by B underneath, at the wrist, the elbow and the armpit. The cut must be precise and on the right side of the joint for the arm to drop in three sections. A responds, reacting to the contact alone. The drop needs to be instantaneous, felt, and spontaneous, not planned or considered. The tempo of interaction can be increased while still maintaining precision. B's impulse-giving can then be extended to gentle pushes to which A reacts, moving then returning to the relaxed starting point where the impulse first landed.

In addition to such detailed bodywork in pairs, we also created a long massacre sequence, depicting it as a Rabelaisian, carnivalesque, group killing spree. We wanted the audience to experience the frenzy that can overtake a mob, guided by historical descriptions as well as analysis of the play text. Rick Bowers describes the massacre's contradictory complexity as Marlowe wrote it: 'These brief scenes allow for quick entry, execution and exit. Paradoxically, the random, desperate violence which they enact is perceived as joyfully unifying on the part of the perpetrators' (in White, 1997: 136).

A crucial aim for rehearsals was to achieve this cohesion. Along with football crowd-like chants, we utilised vuvuzelas, handbells, football rattles, and cow-bells, following the textual mentions of alarums, trumpets, drums, bell ringing, and musket shots and ordinance being fired (the latter is the signal to start the massacre). I taught the students basic acrobatics and lifts, which enabled some performers to be carried head high in rehearsal improvisations. As we moved and processed, we sang in French the catchy song 'Vive Henry IV, vive ce Roi Vaillant/Long Live Henry IV, Long live this valiant King' (1581). None of this is described in the play text, which has minimal stage directions. Starting from historical sources instead, we allowed our imaginations to run riot, literally.

A further inspiration was Jerzy Grotowski's *The Tragical History of Dr Faustus* (1963), a version of Marlowe's play that was also being presented in our season by another Fourth Monkey cast and director in The Marlowe Theatre Studio. In Grotowski's interpretation, the audience is invited to spend Faustus' last hour and have supper with him, seated at long refectory tables. All sounds are made live by the actors to conjure up birds, wind, dripping water, and supernatural noises.

In the same way, we wished to surround the audience with sound and movement to make them feel immersed in the massacre, as though they too were trapped, unable to flee. The lively acoustics and spaces between, around, and behind the audience could be used to full effect, as actors loudly twirled their rattles and tooted their vuvuzelas while charging amongst the spectators. A Catholic chased a Protestant fleeing across the stage. There was laughter and cheers of joy and celebration as much as screams of terror. We fixed the massacre's staging, without choreographing it as such, to establish the tempo, volume levels, and the coordination of actions with entrances and exits. The physical sequence, with its movement and murders, was punctuated and supported by a complex live sound score, with sporadic text and vocalisations. The actors' freedom in the massacre and its staging came directly out of my physical and vocal choral work in rehearsals, as can be seen in Carver's film.

Our production took place four years after Steve Green had founded Fourth Monkey Drama School. Our approach broadly reflected the school's philosophy of encouraging collaboration, ensemble, and creativity, although it also pushed what could be considered its familiar idiom or playing style into new areas. Eleanor Cotton-Soares, one of the cast of twenty-four, recounts her experience:

> the *Massacre at Paris* rehearsals have got increasingly badly behaved. [...] The sense of 'play' has increased. 'Play' seems like a light term to use in the presence [of] such weighted words, like 'murder', 'rape' and 'sovereignty'. Though for our purpose, and this play, that particular juxtaposition is an absolutely perfect one. The sheer gravity of Massacre as written is brought further into the limelight with the carnivalesque mentality many of the characters employ throughout the deed itself. [...] As a result, this performance is a refreshing one in terms of Fourth Monkey playing. [...] we have recreated a seemingly classical story into something quite extraordinary. (Cotton-Soares, 2014)

Cotton-Soares was highlighting the combination of creative playing and experimentation with realism in terms of the setting and its history, the period costumes and props, and the attempt to make the characters and their deaths believable, even if the murders were done with blunt wooden crucifixes. Much of the play involves political plotting and discussion in difficult verse, but it is nothing without the violence and murders at its heart. Chéreau chose water to underscore the horror; we amplified it through movement and sound, interlinked in the young actors' performances.

One of the few reviews we received described this playful and creative sonic aspect:

> The production also makes some interesting decisions when it comes to sound. Percussion instruments being used out of sight seems baffling at first, particularly the use of a ratchet/football rattle clicking and crackling whenever we encounter violence. It begins sporadically, punctuating kicks, punches and stabs of the dagger, and seems remarkably out of place. By the end of the play, however, as the murders reach a crescendo and the cold, hard,

ancient, crypt floor is littered the [sic] bodies, the rattle has become a character in its own right, used to cleverly raise the tension and highlight the chaos and mayhem of the massacre. (*What's on Stage*, 2014)

The acoustically difficult space, which rendered spoken language hard to hear, forced us to be creative and use live sound, extensive choral movement, and inventive staging strategies, rather than recorded media or static scenes with a focus on text. From my perspective, our success lay in the fact that the process had given a large group of training performers an extraordinary experience in an exceptional space, a chance to bring life to a still-so-resonant historical event, documented and depicted by one of Britain's most significant playwrights. The apparent limitations of this supposedly unperformable play, with its brevity and choppy structure, were instead a gift for experimentation.

Canterbury Cathedral Crypt resonated with the sounds of the past, disturbing its usual holy silence. At one of the four performances, I sat behind two elderly spectators who, when it ended, turned to each other. He said, 'I couldn't see anything'. She swiftly replied, '*I* couldn't hear anything'. According to the popular maxim, the three wise monkeys see, hear, and speak no evil. Perhaps the fourth monkey for these two spectators was, in the shape of this performance, evil personified! No director welcomes such a review, but, in our defence, the couple had fidgeted from the start on the Cathedral's admittedly uncomfortable wooden chairs, probably unprepared for such an unusual event and play text. More reassuringly, although clearly with 'skin in the game', the Cathedral's Dean Willis commented positively in a promotional video (unavailable today) made by The Marlowe Theatre soon afterwards: 'The result was profound'. Whatever the response, an important statement was made about performing an unperformable text on a vital, still highly relevant topic, using movement and sound as the creative engine.

Heart of a Dog

Major Road was founded in 1973 and officially dissolved in 2014. The small company, based in Bradford, UK, made its name in community projects and national touring. I was a full-time movement director for their musical adaptation of *Heart of a Dog*, a short story (1925 [2009]) by Kyiv-born Soviet writer Mikhail Bulgakov. The book was much later adapted by British company Complicité as an opera (*A Dog's Heart*, 2010), though there is no overt connection between the two projects, especially as Complicité used puppetry and masks to depict the dog and dog/human. Our approach focused on the actor's technique rather than visual means to achieve the required transformations.

The novella is set in post-revolutionary Moscow and tells the story of a stray dog, Sharik, who is taken in by the scientist and surgeon Professor Preobrazhensky. He transplants the pituitary gland and testes of a deceased criminal into the dog to create a new supercharged Soviet man. Sharik transforms into a human-like creature but retains many animalistic traits, becoming more coarse, aggressive, and socially disruptive, chasing cats and peeing on the carpet. Disappointed by the result, the Professor eventually reverses the operation, turning Sharik back into a passively obedient mutt.

Our adaptation followed the story closely, although with a tiny comic chorus formed from the cast of five, who observed and commented on the action, often through song. Like the book, the piece used humour to question aspects of Soviet ideology and practice, and Stalin and Stalinism. The script, which I cite and refer to here, is dated 21 December 1990, almost a year to the day before the Soviet Union was officially dissolved as a sovereign state under Mikhail Gorbachev's leadership. The performance premiered in February 1991. Our critique was therefore topical.

More than any other production discussed so far, Gardzienice's exercises and approach could be incorporated almost without change into the rehearsal process. This is partly because the piece was a musical adaptation with a chorus, with protagonists emerging from and then returning to the group, in a dramaturgical pattern that echoed the structure of Gardzienice's performances, which themselves were inspired by religious worship and Ancient Greek drama. Our approach demanded musicality, close rhythmical ensemble work, and the radical transformation by actor Jem Wall from a speaking dog into a dog/man and then back to a dog. This suited the highly energetic Gardzienice training.

Interestingly, Wall had, like Mitchell, and at the same time, received Winston Churchill Memorial Trust funding to research theatre and acting in Georgia and Russia, where he had seen a production of *Heart of a Dog*. He had then brought the idea of staging the novella to Dix and Major Road. Although his fieldwork was geographically distant from mine, like Mitchell and I, Wall was looking for a different kind of acting from familiar British approaches, one that was not about empty 'style', as he characterised it, but which required an actor's total physical commitment. He also wanted acting to have social/political meaning (Dix and Wall interview, 2025). He and I had worked together on *Arden*, and he had recommended me for this project. This connection and our shared interests, concerns, and experience allowed us to lead movement work together and hit the ground running with a familiar vocabulary. The principle of mutuality was reinforced by our previous interactions.

Wall's acting task was to depict the results of a grotesque scientific experiment, which led regressively to doggy behaviours emerging spontaneously from an otherwise normal Soviet human being, albeit a criminal, drunk one. This case study is stylistically a long way from the naturalism of much of Mitchell's work at that time, although the role had aspects in common with the possession in *The Dybbuk* that would follow a year later. There were even affinities with Rachel's 'possession' and the animalistic characteristics of the Travellers in *Live Like Pigs* (1993), explored in Section 1. *The Dybbuk* would focus on attempting as realistic a transformation as possible, but here my role as movement director was to help create an absurd grotesque aesthetic, drawing more from Vsevolod Meyerhold than Konstantin Stanislavsky, in terms of Bulgakov's two theatre contemporaries. Wall had studied Drama at the University of Bristol under Meyerhold scholar Ted Braun, which helped to inform our approach. Braun was, though, also an expert on naturalism. Wall wanted his portrayal to be convincing, grounded, and truthful, however exaggerated, stylised, or expressive the form. He tried to combine animalistic spontaneity and impulse with rationality.

My involvement in rehearsals was focused on two tasks: first, to create choral movement sequences; second, to establish the dog's and then the dog/man's behaviour and movements. The two elements then had to be integrated. Gardzienice's physical work emphasises moving from the centre, always grounded but with a relaxed upper body. The nature of the Professor's operation and the piece's focus on sexualised and scatological behaviour meant that there was a natural synergy between the training and the text.

Wall worked on lowering his centre of gravity, combined with quick, impulsive leaps. A jump drawn from Japanese Kabuki proved useful – kneeling on the floor with the back upright and knees together, in a split second, the performer leaps to a crouch, sweeping their legs out from underneath them, pulling up rapidly from the centre. This then led to a dog-like Cossack dance. The chorus describes how 'the dog rose up on his hind legs in front of Philip Philipovich and bowed before him' (*Heart of a Dog*, 1990: 12). A page later, Sharik does another doggy dance when he sniffs some food prepared for him. A useful source for Wall was Desmond Morris' *Dogwatching* (1987). Such actions grew from movement explorations and group play, as well as one-to-one work between Wall and me. A group improvisation, where the cast all played dogs, generated multiple ideas. The process was extremely collaborative and always centred on ensemble work. Dix was a very inclusive director.

Gardzienice's training includes different ways of walking, always from the centre, one of which involves a very animated, swirling, close-knit group walk, which stops on a count of four (Allain, 1997: 62, and Plate 1b). This is then interspersed with pair exercises before the group walks again, all orchestrated through the breath. The walk is linked to emphatic, rhythmical breathing, exaggerated and audible. This exercise helped the chorus to move and halt in tableaux, operating as a tight ensemble. To breathwork, we added vocalisation. In Gardzienice's *Carmina Burana* (1990), the song *Ave formosissima* (Praise be to the greatest) is used heavily adapted from Carl Orff's choral piece on which the performance was partly based. We took these two Latin words and improvised with voice and movement, emphasising either vowels or consonants.

Some of the script was to be sung, mainly by the chorus, including words such as 'Sausage' (*Heart of a Dog*, 1990: 2–3), used at the start to lure Sharik to the Professor's house. We savoured playing with such text, satirising operatic conventions with spoof seriousness. The chorus sang: 'The dog gathered up his last remaining strength. Sausage! And crawled out of the gutter, onto the pavement. Sausage!' (*Heart of a Dog*, 1990: 3). We explored rhythmically the complex Russian names with their patronymics to familiarise and thus 'own' them, but also to investigate their sounds. Philip Philipovich Preobrazhensky became a musical tongue twister. By reciting the words 'violin, viola, and cello', we encouraged the use of head (violin), throat, and chest (viola), and then chest and lower resonators (cello), respectively, grounding vocal vibration in the body. This, in turn, amplified the voice and fitted well with actor Judith Brydon's onstage playing of the cello. We worked with names across the resonators, part of our highly physicalised, integrated voice, music, and movement approach.

The team, with me and musical director Lawrie Wright working under Dix's watchful eye, attempted to make the whole cohere by focusing on rhythm and musicality. Much of the text was spoken, but usually in short sections or single lines. Sometimes there were politically nuanced, longer speeches, but such dialogue was often interrupted by other characters, the dog's misbehaviour, or choral commentary, much of it sung. The piece flowed at a fast pace, brought alive by either the comic antics of the dog or dog/man, the citizens' battles with the state, or absurd scenes from 'real life' that exposed the inequities that existed in a supposedly equal society.

Some of the action was almost cartoon-like, basic clowning. Comedy is not something one associates with Gardzienice's work and the Polish tradition, but this shows how training practices such as basic acrobatics and rhythmical work can cut across forms and genres. The training can be applied in multiple contexts. A review from Portsmouth noted that the chase scenes were reminiscent of the Keystone Cops films, and commented on how the production 'mixed gymnastics, operatics and music' (*The News*, 1991). The small cast had to be energetic, shifting between physical enactment, such as showing a swirling wind, sharply defined individual characterisation, or choral movement and music, which either pushed the narrative forward or commented on events.

The News also described how Wall 'gave us an extremely convincing portrayal of a flea-bitten hound right down to the last scratch' (1991). John Shaw wrote of the opening performance in Bradford that there was 'Excellent believable acting by all the cast' (*Northern Star*, 1991). This was not naturalism by any definition, but the production still relied on precise observation, imitation, and wholehearted enactment. We were clear that the darkness and pain in the story, its grotesque aspect, also had to be brought out. The dog's situation and hurt must be felt and not just be a source of humour. The fusion of precise naturalistic acting and formal stylisation is reminiscent of what Mitchell and I were later to explore in *The Machine Wreckers*, a production in which Wall also acted.

Conclusion

Analysis of these three productions has shown how movement practices can be deployed for creative purposes in text-based performances and that they are vital for enacting violence and death. They are useful for devising choral work, especially with a musical, sonic, or rhythmical dimension. Analysis of the process used for *Heart of a Dog* has reinforced how movement in rehearsal can help the actor perform radical transformations, in this instance into an animal, followed by an animal/human hybrid, and then back again. This is not of the same order as *The Dybbuk*'s possession, but rather the outcome of fantastical science, even if the endpoints and aspects of the process were similar. For the actors involved, the spontaneous eruption of Khonen's voice and actions from Leye's abused body has affinities with doggy behaviour unexpectedly emerging from Preobrazhensky's new Soviet 'man'.

In earlier sections, I described how specific behavioural characteristics, patterns, and even atmospheres could be brought to life and realised on stage through careful spatial movement investigations in rehearsals. In *Massacre*, beyond the very specific textual requirement to depict so many murders and deaths, the performance space posed many challenges. Some of these, such as the acoustic difficulties, could not be reconciled with the means available. Other demands could be answered – through movement. From my perspective, these challenges were addressed positively, with creativity and innovation.

What succeeds in Poland does not translate easily to a British context. The choices we made for *Henry* around the staging, the choral links between scenes, the creation of an early modern culture, and the forging of a strong ensemble, all informed by Gardzienice's practice, were appreciated by audiences and critics alike. Yet the voice work received mixed reviews.

My input as movement director could have little bearing on this aspect of the production, but in more general terms, how movement relates to speaking needs further investigation. Here, I have only mentioned some problems and small explorations, rather than proposing worked-out solutions. Questions about the relationship between vocal/textual delivery and movement aside, it is evident that movement is vital in theatre-making. Yet it needs to be said, as a final cautionary note, that the increasing use of personal microphones will only diminish further the body's role in textual delivery.

Conclusion: Lessons from Polish Practice

This Element has shown that there are ways of considering and describing movement's position in relation to acting and performance, which extend beyond narrative, stories, language, and texts. In some performance forms, movement may indeed function as a base with which to tell stories, perhaps in a literal, representational way. Yet possibilities reach so much further. Movement practices are imaginatively constrained if always framed in linguistic or even representational terms. In *Movement Direction* (2022), Kate Flatt uses the term 'physical narratives', part of the book's subtitle. Ayse Tashkiran frequently mentions 'physical language' in her 2020 collection of interviews. Advocating for the significance of movement in theatre is not best served by terms that default to or replicate textual or linguistic models.

Movement work sits adjacent to a given text or texts, responding to, interpreting, questioning, and challenging them. It also exists outside and beyond them, offering creative choices for the actor or director which pertain as much to spatial arrangements and patterns (an important, recurring consideration in this Element), individual and collective stage behaviours, personal or choral rhythms and music, or a whole world of other possibilities. Movement can, for example, assist with the forging of an ensemble, however elusive a concept this may be.

At its most fundamental level, movement supports acting and characterisation. It helps actors exist and move together, stand, listen, and respond on stage. It creates and is a central part of what Mitchell calls the 'world of the play'. Unlike Githa Sowerby, with her complex and detailed stage directions, many playwrights do not explain or indicate movement choices or actions in their texts. Some plays may be corrupt or incomplete, or they may be adapted and evolve collaboratively. Much is left to be discovered in rehearsals. This archaeological work can be done or led by the movement director, inspired by both legible and imagined prompts.

It is pleasing that this specialist role has now earned its place in rehearsals and professional theatre, as well as in higher education. There is a small but growing number of Master's courses in the UK that focus on movement directing. These did not exist over thirty years ago when I was working in this area, just as the role itself then appeared rarely in British text-based theatre. Movement directors are everywhere today, though with shrinking arts budgets, this could well change. The labour of movement has become visible, even if some of its key proponents, such as Struan Leslie, argue for its invisibility, at least on stage.

To some extent, Leslie is correct to focus on movement's absence, as it relates not just to what an audience can see or notice: in fights, dances, riots, protests, murders, deaths, possessions, exorcisms, fist-banging, other scripted physical interactions, or perhaps for framing a production or the linking of scenes. It is also about what happens in stillness or between actors, what occurs in the body sometimes at the smallest level, in minute, almost imperceptible breathing changes. Movement can be about what is held back, impulses that are not acted upon. Stillness is a vital part of movement, however paradoxical this might at first seem.

An aspect that has appeared across these case studies is the actor's requirement to enact some kind of possession or radical transformation: whether this is caused by the invasion of another's soul, is a manifestation of a character's behaviour, or results from impossible surgery. One-to-one movement sessions can help actors with what can seem a daunting task. In the pressurised, short rehearsal periods of British theatre, a director might rarely find time to conduct detailed work on these transformations. Delegation of such explorations to a movement director is a sensible use of expertise and time. The same applies to the complex act of killing or dying on stage, or to stage violence, tasks that should never be underestimated.

Acting frequently has an ethical dimension, especially when the transformation involves cultural, religious, or temporal shifts, as Section 1 described. Movement can help address ethical issues and the complexities of representation through detailed, practical research that grounds characters in precise facts or evidence, perhaps to create verisimilitude. It strives to avoid caricatures, clichés, misrepresentations or falsities. In Mitchell's naturalistic productions, responsibility for this is strongly foregrounded and keenly defended. Critics have noted and celebrated this aspect, even as they simultaneously recognise and bemoan related problems, most repeatedly some actors' inaudibility.

Vocal delivery is a topic that is too often ignored in studies of movement. Movement scholars often say little about voice or regard texts mostly in terms of how they might inform non-verbal movement, gesture or body language. Flatt hardly mentions it in her definition and account of movement directing and the work a movement director does, beyond speaking about an 'audio environment which may include music' (Flatt, 2022: 13). Live voice is almost absent, apart from a dedicated section on movement directing in opera, where, though, the focus is on singing rather than speaking. Sometimes breath is discussed, but usually only concerning movement rather than text or vocal delivery. This is especially surprising since Flatt has been a movement director for Mitchell. In her Themes section, Tashkiran states that 'Movement supports engagement with the text and has to work in harmony with the way a performer uses their voice' (Tashkiran, 2020: 30). This is as far as it goes. There is, then, a noticeable lack, especially from the perspective of the specific lineage of Polish theatre that I scoped briefly in the introduction, where voice and body are integrated and recorded music is rarely used. Movement's potential is enriched by reflecting on the voice and textual delivery.

I have tried, in this Element, to address such exclusions and reconfigure, through examples drawn from my own experience, the emphasis on text-oriented language in dominant movement discourses. I have highlighted the influence that Polish movement and acting practices have had on British theatre. Even though some specific exercises have not been taken directly from Polish practices, such as chi kung or other martial arts, my use of them in British rehearsals has been inspired by that theatre's prioritisation of the body. This emphasis on physicality first is one of the most important considerations that we can take from this cultural source. Another is the need to integrate voice and body work.

With its auto-ethnographic approach, this Element has focused narrowly on my professional work, connected through this to Mitchell in particular, Gardzienice to a large extent, and Grotowski to a lesser degree. A richer story needs to be told about Polish experimental theatre's influence on British practices, and not just in terms of movement. Many theatre artists worked with Grotowski and his collaborators in the 1970s and 1980s, including, as just two examples, Tim Crouch and Mike Pearson of Brith Gof, the latter of whom very actively discussed and explored this connection. Others worked with Gardzienice, when I was there (like Rice) or after I left in 1993, including Anna-Helena McLean. Alison Hodge's substantial interactions with the company have been recorded in her writings (Hodge, 2004) and a DVD (Hodge, 2013). Later, Niamh Dowling, current Principal of RADA, London, collaborated closely with Song of the Goat, as documented in her 2011 article. In another connection, Ian Morgan, who runs the MA Theatre Laboratory at RADA, was a member of the Workcentre of Jerzy Grotowski and Thomas Richards in

Pontedera, Italy, during the Art as vehicle phase, though it is debatable to what extent this is 'Polish'. Even if these influences have been documented or analysed, they are often not defined in relation to movement specifically. Taking these artists and teachers together, alongside my own reflections, a picture emerges about a relatively undocumented but complex strand of influence from Poland on British theatre.

It is worth noting that, except for *Heart of a Dog*, where I had some input into the adaptation during rehearsals, in this Element I have only analysed work on pre-existing, whole play texts. In other forms, such as devising, physical theatre, or dance theatre, the role movement plays is even more substantial. This is, though, a topic for another book. I hope that this Element has introduced a slice of unexplored theatre history that can inspire others (academics, students, and theatre artists) to reconsider the value and place of movement as a creative and training tool for all kinds of theatre- and performance-making. The Polish influence is just a small part of this bigger picture.

I have only briefly mentioned how the movement director relates to other artistic positions, including the director. With *Massacre*, my input extended into co-directing. Similarly, with Mitchell, I worked on two productions as assistant or co-director, one of which was not even mentioned here (*Diarmuid and Graine*, rural Poland, 1991). This exclusion is because it does not fit this Element's parameters, as it was an unusual, cross-cultural, rural touring experiment that has few comparison or connection points. Even when it was not formally articulated in such a way, my role with Mitchell often seemed more akin to that of an assistant director. Sometimes I was in all rehearsals and in constant dialogue, including on the phone after rehearsals finished at 10 PM. This is not to claim authorship or recognition, rather to emphasise how vital movement can be to theatre-making. Perhaps this is not surprising: my analysis here has encompassed acting, transformation, space, ensemble, voice, music, text, and the world of the play.

It seems appropriate to give the final word to two practitioners: one of the UK's most celebrated actors, cited by a renowned critic discussing Mitchell's work. In his review of her *Ghosts*, Paul Taylor quotes Simon Russell Beale, who played Oswald and described her rehearsal process as 'phenomenally rigorous'. Taylor takes this further, suggesting that 'Her tireless research suggests a passionate need to feel that drama has direct access to non-theatrical life' (*Independent*, 1994). For all of us, not just Mitchell, movement offers a way of seeing and being in the world, not just for the stage. As we walk, run, sit, or quietly think, however active or still we might be, let this not be forgotten.

References

Abramowicz, M., Ciechowicz, J. and Kręglewska-Powązka, K. (eds.) (2017) *Dybuk: na pograniczu dwóch światów/The Dybbuk: In Between Two Worlds*. Gdańsk: Wydawnictwo Uniwersytetu Gdańskiego.

Allain, P. (1994) 'Movement Directing', *Total Theatre*, Winter 6–4(9). https://totaltheatre.org.uk/archive/features/movement-directing (Accessed: 21 July 2025).

Allain, P. (1997) *Gardzienice: Polish Theatre in Transition*. Amsterdam: Taylor & Francis.

Allain, P. and Camilleri, F. (2018) *Physical Actor Training – an Online A–Z*. Bloomsbury, Methuen Drama films online. www.dramaonlinelibrary.com/physical-actor-training (Accessed: 23 July 2025).

Allain, P. (2020) 'Stumbling around Polish Theatre with Katie Mitchell: A Personal Reflection', *Contemporary Theatre Review*, Special Issue on Katie Mitchell, 30(2), 260–264.

Allain, P. (2023) 'Filming Process: Questions and Considerations', *Theatre, Dance and Performance Training*, 14(4), 431–443.

An-sky, Sh. (1992) *The Dybbuk*. Personal Rehearsal Copy.

Arden, J. (2014) *Arden Plays 1: Waters of Babylon; When Is a Door ...; Live Like Pigs; Serjeant Musgrave's Dance; The Happy Haven*. London: Bloomsbury Publishing.

Britton, J. (ed.) (2013) *Encountering Ensemble*. London: Bloomsbury Publishing.

Bulgakov, M. (2009) *The Heart of a Dog*. London: Random House.

Campo, G. and Molik, Z. (2010) *Zygmunt Molik's Voice and Body Work: The Legacy of Jerzy Grotowski*. Abingdon: Routledge.

Caplan, D. and Moss, R. M. (2023) *The Dybbuk Century*. Michigan: University of Michigan Press.

Carver, G. (2016) *Bodies in the Crypt: A Director's Perspective*. Routledge Performance Archive. www.routledgeperformancearchive.com/browse/commentators/paul-allain/bodies-in-the-crypt-by-paul-allain (Accessed: 6 May 2025). Film.

Chang, H. (2016) *Autoethnography as Method*. New York: Taylor and Francis.

Cheney, P. (ed.) (2006) *Cambridge Companion to Christopher Marlowe*. Cambridge: Cambridge University Press.

Cornford, T. and Svich, C. (eds.) (2020) *Contemporary Theatre Review*, Special Issue on Katie Mitchell, 30(2), 135–302.

References

Cotton-Soares, E. (2014) Notes on *Massacre at Paris* rehearsals. Other.

Denzin, N. (2013) *Interpretive Autoethnography*. London: SAGE Publications.

Dowling, N. (2011) 'Teatr Piesn Kozla and its Integration into Western European Theatre Training', *Theatre, Dance and Performance Training*, 2(2), 243–259.

Evans, M. (2009) *Movement Training for the Modern Actor*. London: Taylor & Francis.

Evans, M. (2019) *Performance, Movement and the Body*. London: Bloomsbury Publishing.

Evans, S. (2004) *Stopping Places: A Gypsy History of South London and Kent*. Hertfordshire: University of Hertfordshire Press.

Fensham, R. (2021) *Theory for Theatre Studies: Movement*. London: Bloomsbury Publishing.

Flatt, K. (2022) *Movement Direction: Developing Physical Narrative for Performance*. Marlborough: The Crowood Press.

Fowler, B. (ed.) (2018) *The Theatre of Katie Mitchell*. London: Routledge.

Fowler, B. (2021) *Katie Mitchell: Beautiful Illogical Acts*. Abingdon: Taylor & Francis.

Gottlieb, V. (2005) 'Vakhtangov's Musicality: Reassessing Yevgeny Vakhtangov (1883–1922)', *Contemporary Theatre Review*, 15(2), 259–268.

Green D. and Ewan V. (2015) *Actor Movement: Expression of the Physical Being*. London: Bloomsbury Academic.

Grotowski, J. (1968) *Towards a Poor Theatre*. London: Methuen.

Harvie, J. (2005) *Staging the UK*. Manchester: Manchester University Press.

Hodge, A. (2013) *Core Training for the Relational Actor*. London: Routledge. DVD.

Hodge, A. and Staniewski, W. (2004) *Hidden Territories: The Theatre of Gardzienice*. London: Routledge. With DVD.

Ibsen, H. (2014) *Ibsen Plays 1: Ghosts; The Wild Duck; The Master Builder*. London: Bloomsbury Publishing.

Kennedy, D. (1964) *English Folk Dancing: Today and Yesterday*. London: Harper-Collins.

Kershaw, B. and Nicholson, H. (eds) (2011) *Research Methods in Theatre and Performance*. Edinburgh: Edinburgh University Press.

Kurosawa, A. (1954) *Seven Samurai*. Japan: Toho Co., Ltd. Film.

Landis, J. (ed.) (1966) *3 Great Jewish Plays*. New York: Applause.

Major Road. *Heart of a Dog*. (1990) Personal Rehearsal Copy.

Marlowe, C. (2003) (ed. J. B. Steane) *The Complete Plays*. London: Penguin Classics.

References

Mitchell, K. (2009) *The Director's Craft: A Handbook for the Theatre*. London: Taylor & Francis.

Pitches, J., Murray, S., Poynor, H. and Worth, L. et al. (2011) 'Performer Training: Researching Practice in the Theatre Laboratory', in Kershaw, B. and Nicholson, H. (eds.) *Research Methods in Theatre and Performance*. Edinburgh: Edinburgh University Press. pp. 137–161.

Quigley, K. (2020) *Performing the Unstageable*. London: Methuen

Radosavljević, D. (ed.) (2013) *The Contemporary Ensemble*. London: Routledge.

Radosavljević, D. (2020) 'Curating the Invisible: An Archive-Embedded Interview with Struan Leslie', *Contemporary Theatre Review*. (2020) Special Issue on Katie Mitchell, 30(2), 236–244.

Russell Taylor, J. (1963) *Anger and After*. Harmondsworth: Pelican.

Shakespeare, W. (2008) *The Oxford Shakespeare: Henry VI Part Three*. Oxford: Oxford University Press.

Solga, K. and Rebellato, D. (2018) 'Katie Mitchell and the Politics of Naturalist Theatre', in Fowler, B. (ed.) *The Theatre of Katie Mitchell*. London: Routledge. pp. 39–71.

Sowerby, G. (1994) *Rutherford and Son*. Personal Rehearsal Copy.

Tashkiran, A. (2020) *Movement Directors in Contemporary Theatre: Conversations on Craft*. London: Bloomsbury Publishing.

Taylor, G., Jowett, J., Bourus, T., and Egan, G. (eds.) (2016) *The New Oxford Shakespeare: Modern Critical Edition*. Oxford: Oxford University Press.

Tinius, J. (2024) 'Fieldwork as Method in Theatre and Performance Studies', in Davis, T. C. and Rae, P. (eds.) *The Cambridge Guide to Mixed Methods Research for Theatre and Performance Studies*. Cambridge: Cambridge University Press. pp. 190–212.

Toller, E. (1936) *Seven Plays by Ernst Toller*. New York: Liveright Publishing Corporation.

White, P. (ed.) (1997) *Marlowe, History and Sexuality*. New York: AMS Press.

Interview

11 July 2025. On *Heart of a Dog* with Al Dix (director) and Jem Wall (actor).

Websites Referenced

Atkinson, J. B. (1926) *The Dybbuk*. Review in the *New York Times*, 14 December. https://muse.jhu.edu/pub/166/oa_monograph/chapter/3769977 (Accessed: 21 August 2025).

BBC (2021) 'Gypsy, Roma and Traveller Performers "Under-Represented" on-screen'. www.bbc.co.uk/news/uk-northern-ireland-55419654 (Accessed: 6 May 2025).

Billington, M. (2023) 'Ibsen's *Ghosts*'. www.theguardian.com/stage/2023/nov/06/ibsen-ghosts-productions (Accessed: 21 August 2025).

Boyd, M. (2010) 'RSC and Ensemble'. www.youtube.com/watch?v=ogKjPpQQyn8&t=19s (Accessed: 6 May 2025).

Christon, L. (1994) 'She Delivers More than a Message'. www.latimes.com/archives/la-xpm-1994-10-30-ca-56527-story.html (Accessed: 6 May 2025).

Freedman, H. (2019) 'How to Deal with a Dybbuk'. www.thejc.com/judaism/how-to-deal-with-a-dybbuk-p3c4sgkb (Accessed: 11 March 2025).

Higgins, C. (2016) 'Katie Mitchell, British Theatre's Queen in Exile', *Guardian*. www.theguardian.com/stage/2016/jan/14/british-theatre-queen-exile-katie-mitchell (Accessed: 17 July 2025).

Kafrissen, R. (2022) 'The Many Faces of *The Dybbuk*'. www.tabletmag.com/sections/community/articles/many-faces-dybbuk (Accessed: 10 June 2025).

Lumet, S. (1960) '*The Dybbuk*'. www.youtube.com/watch?v=Y4zM0cyHmdc (Accessed: 6 May 2025).

Maman, S. (no date) 'Dance Website'. www.israelidances.com/choreographer.asp?name=shlomomaman (Accessed: 6 May 2025).

Mitchell, K. (1995) 'Weavers of Dreams'. *Independent*. www.independent.co.uk/arts-entertainment/weavers-of-dreams-1593259.html (Accessed: 6 May 2025).

Museum of the Yiddish Theatre (no date) '*The Dybbuk*'. www.museumoffamilyhistory.com/moyt/pih/habima-dybbuk.htm (Accessed: 6 May 2025).

Pfefferman, N. (2003) 'Polish Director Honors Legacy with Classic Tale'. https://jewishjournal.com/culture/arts/8212/ (Accessed: 12 June 2025).

Posner, D. N. (2023) 'Documents on the Creation and Reception of Habima's *the Dybbuk*'. https://muse.jhu.edu/pub/166/oa_monograph/chapter/3769977 (Accessed: 6 May 2025).

The Stage (2025) 'Fagin Actor Simon Lipkin: Jewish Roles Can Be Played by Anyone "If Done with Respect"'. www.thestage.co.uk/news/fagin-actor-simon-lipkin-jewish-roles-can-be-played-by-anyone-if-done-with-respect (Accessed: 6 May 2025).

Wagner, J. (2023) 'We Need to Talk about Jewface'. www.thejc.com/life/we-need-to-talk-about-jewface-k10jdsj5 (Accessed: 6 May 2025).

Wagner, J. (no date) 'Casting Jewish'. https://juliawagnerfilm.com/castingjewish/ (Accessed: 6 May 2025).

William Hogarth Etching (no date) 'Hudibras Encounters the Skimmington'. www.rct.uk/collection/913465/hudibras-encounters-the-skimmington (Accessed: 18 May 2025).

Archives

Major Road Archive, University of Leeds, Leeds. https://explore.library.leeds.ac.uk/special-collections-explore/609645/major_road_theatre_collection.

Platform on *Rutherford and Son*, 3 June 1994, Royal National Theatre Archive, London. www.nationaltheatre.org.uk/about-us/archive/.

Royal Court Living Archive, 2023. https://livingarchive.royalcourttheatre.com/plays/live-like-pigs-2/.

Royal Shakespeare Archive, Shakespeare Birthplace Trust, Stratford-upon-Avon. https://collections.shakespeare.org.uk/search/everything.

Exhibition

The Dybbuk: Phantom of the Lost World (2024–2025), Museum of the Art and History of Judaism, Paris. September 2024 – January 2025.

Cited Production Reviews in Chronological Order

Collected Reviews of all productions except *Heart of a Dog* and *The Massacre at Paris* are available by subscription through the *Theatre Record* archive: www.theatrerecord.com/magazine/archive (Accessed: 17 August 2025).

1990

Arden of Faversham

Christy, D. *Guardian*, 13 August.
Letts, Q. *Daily Telegraph*, 13 August.
Macaulay, A. *Financial Times*, 13 August.
Robertson, N. *Time Out*, 15 August.
Wearing, K. *City Limits*, 16 August.

Vassa Zheleznova

Billington, M. *Guardian*, 19 November.

1991

Heart of A Dog

Shaw, J. *Northern Star*, 14 February.
Unknown. *The News* (Portsmouth), 21 February.

1992

The Dybbuk

Billington, M. *Guardian*, 16 July.
Morley, S. *Herald Tribune*, 22 July.
Shuttleworth, I. *City Limits*. www.cix.co.uk/~shutters/reviews/92075.htm (Accessed: 6 May 2025).
Taylor, P. 'Spirit of the Moment', *Independent*, 15 July. www.independent.co.uk/arts-entertainment/theatre-spirit-of-the-moment-paul-taylor-on-the-rsc-s-production-of-anski-s-the-dybbuk-1533537.html (Accessed: 6 May 2025).
Woddis, C. *What's On*, 22 July.

1993

Ghosts

Billington, M. *Guardian*, 14 June.
Ingram, M. 'Recreating Past World of Hypocrisy', *Stratford Herald*, 18 June.
Macaulay, A. *Financial Times*, 12 June.
Peter, J. 'Fear Eats the Soul', *Sunday Times*, 20–23 June.
Spencer, C. *Daily Telegraph*, 14 June.

Live Like Pigs

Christopher, J. *Time Out*, 27 October.
Coveney, M. *Observer*, 24 October.
Doughty, L. *Mail on Sunday*, 31 October.
Wiegand, C. (2016) 'Royal Court at 60', 24 March. www.theguardian.com/stage/2016/mar/24/the-royal-court-at-60-look-back-in-wonder (Accessed: 6 May 2025).

1994

Rutherford and Son

Billington, M. *Guardian*, 4 June.
de Jongh, N. *Evening Standard*, 3 June, p. 7.
Peter, J. *Sunday Times*, 12 June, p. 20.
Taylor, P. *Independent*, 4 June.
Wardle, I. *Independent on Sunday*, 5 June.

Henry VI: The Battle for the Throne

Barker, N. 'Not a Trouser in Sight', *Observer*, 14 August.
Gore-Langton, R. 'Rare Gem Found in Battle for the Crown', *Daily Telegraph*, 15 August, p. 15.
Taylor, P (b). 'An Eye for the Small Print', *Independent*, 9 August. www.independent.co.uk/arts-entertainment/theatre-an-eye-for-the-small-print-katie-mitchell-has-chosen-to-cut-her-shakespearian-teeth-on-henry-vi-part-3-paul-taylor-analyses-a-young-director-s-decisionmaking-process-1382536.html (Accessed: 6 May 2025).

1995

The Machine Wreckers

Billington, M. *Guardian*, 14 August.
Carlson, M. (1996) 'Katie Mitchell's "The Machine Wreckers"', *Western European Stages*, 7(3), 57–58.
de Jongh, N. *Evening Standard*, 14 August.
Hornby, R. *The Hudson Review*, p. 645.
Peter, J. *Sunday Times*, 20 August.

2014

The Massacre at Paris

Shaw, M. *What's on Stage*, 28 March.

Acknowledgements

I am indebted to Fintan Walsh, Duška Radosavljević, and Caridad Svich for accepting my proposal and their generous feedback to make it more precise. Emily Hockley from CUP kindly stepped in with useful notes and encouragement.

I am grateful to Adam Ledger and Liz Shafer, referees for my successful Society for Theatre Research funding application for archive visits. I warmly thank STR and the two Kates for their assistance with an admirably light bureaucratic process. Staff in the University of Leeds Libraries Cultural Collections, the Royal National Theatre Archive, and the Shakespeare Birthplace Trust Collections team were all very helpful.

Al Dix and Jem Wall gave me their precious time as we blew some collective dust off our memories in an interview. Juliet Chambers-Coe read a draft and encouraged me along the way. Thank you, Juliet.

Thank you to the University of Kent for honouring their commitment to give me study leave, even in very tough times. And as always with leave, I am grateful to my fantastic drama colleagues for making it possible.

For Ukraine

About the Author

Paul Allain is Professor of Theatre and Performance at the University of Kent, UK. He has worked as a Movement Director and actor trainer and has published extensively on actor training and contemporary performance. He has been awarded a medal by the Polish government for promoting Polish culture overseas.

Cambridge Elements

Contemporary Performance Texts

Senior Editor
Fintan Walsh
Birkbeck, University of London

Fintan Walsh is Professor of Performing Arts and Humanities at Birkbeck, University of London, where he is Head of the School of Creative Arts, Culture and Communication and Director of Birkbeck Centre for Contemporary Theatre. He is a former Senior Editor of *Theatre Research International*.

Associate Editors
Duška Radosavljević
Royal Central School of Speech and Drama, University of London

Duška Radosavljević is a Professorial Research Fellow at the Royal Central School of Speech and Drama. Her work has received the David Bradby Research Prize (2015), the Elliott Hayes Award for Dramaturgy (2022) and the ATHE-ASTR Award for Digital Scholarship

Caridad Svich
Rutgers University

Caridad Svich is a playwright and translator. She teaches creative writing and playwriting in the English Department at Rutgers University-New Brunswick.

Advisory Board
Siân Adiseshiah, *Loughborough University*
Helena Grehan, *Murdoch University*
Ameet Parameswaran, *Jawaharlal Nehru University*
Synne Behrndt, *Stockholm University of the Arts*
Jay Pather, *University of Cape Town*
Sodja Zupanc Lotker, *The Academy of Performing Arts in Prague (DAMU)*
Peter M. Boenisch, *Aarhus University*
Hayato Kosuge, *Keio University*
Edward Ziter, *NYU Tisch School of the Arts*
Milena Gras Kleiner, *Pontificia Universidad Católica de Chile*
Savas Patsalidis, *Aristotle University, Thessaloniki, Greece*
Harvey Young, *College of Fine Arts, Boston University*

About the Series
Contemporary Performance Texts responds to the evolution of the form, role and meaning of text in theatre and performance in the late twentieth and twenty-first centuries, by publishing Elements that explore the generation of text for performance, its uses in performance, and its varied modes of reception and documentation.

Cambridge Elements⁼

Contemporary Performance Texts

Elements in the Series

Playwriting, Dramaturgy and Space
Sara Freeman

Performing Grief in Pandemic Theatres
Fintan Walsh

Theatricality, Playtexts and Society
David Barnett

The Poetics of Performance Diagrams
Andrej Mirčev

Comedy and Controversy: Scripting Public Speech
Sarah Balkin and Marc Mierowsky

English Play Development under Neoliberalism, 2000–2022
Lucy Tyler

Movement, Text, Performance
Paul Allain

A full series listing is available at: www.cambridge.org/ECTX

For EU product safety concerns, contact us at Calle de José Abascal, 56–1°,
28003 Madrid, Spain or eugpsr@cambridge.org.

www.ingramcontent.com/pod-product-compliance
Lightning Source LLC
LaVergne TN
LVHW011855060526
838200LV00054B/4348